From Chains to Roses

The Unbreakable Spirit

and

Life of Josephine Margaret Bakhita

By

Mirella Patzer

Copyright

History and Women Press

From Chains to Roses

Second Edition

http://www.mirellapatzer.com

This is a work of fiction. Names, characters, places, and incidents either are the product of the author's imagination or are used fictitiously and any resemblance to actual persons, living or dead, business establishments, events, or location is entirely coincidental. The characters and events portrayed in this book are fictitious and used factiously. Apart from well-known historical figures, any similarity to real persons, living or dead is purely coincidental and not intended by the author.

This is a publication of History and Women Press

https://www.historyandwomen.com

https://www.mirellapatzer.com

Also by Mirella Patzer

Lady of Monza

The Emerald Conspiracy

Her Secret Legacy

Black Petals

The Prophetic Queen

Orphan of the Olive Tree

The Novice

Dangerous Liaisons (A Modern Translation)

FROM CHAINS TO ROSES

The Unforgettable Story of Josephine Bakhita

Some are born into darkness only to become bearers of the most extraordinary light...

Snatched from her village in a violent raid, nine-year-old Bakhita is thrust into a living nightmare. Her identity stripped away, her body carved with 144 brutal scars, she is sold from master to master across the merciless deserts of Sudan. They call her "fortunate one" in cruel mockery, never suspecting the indomitable fire that burns behind her eyes.

In this electrifying, heart-pounding novel, Mirella Patzer throws readers into the savage world of the 19th-century slave trade and the astonishing journey of one woman who refused to be broken by it. When a twist of fate delivers Bakhita to Venice, she discovers something more powerful than her chains, her own voice.

Defying her wealthy "owners" in a sensational court battle that stuns Italian society, Bakhita claims not only her freedom but embarks on a transformation so radical it will leave everyone who encounters her forever changed. As Sister Josephine, her scarred hands become instruments of healing, her hard-won wisdom a balm for the wounded, and her presence a living testament to the possibility of light emerging from the darkest places.

From Chains to Roses is not merely historical fiction. It's an adrenaline shot to the soul. The author's vivid prose drives this explosive narrative forward delivering the emotional impact of an intimate confession. You'll find yourself holding your breath, clenching your fists, and ultimately weeping as Bakhita's extraordinary metamorphosis unfolds.

Prepare to be shattered, inspired, and utterly transformed by the true story of the enslaved girl who became a saint, proving that sometimes the most powerful revolutions begin in the most unlikely hearts.

Dedication

For

Josephine Marasco DiGiacomo

and a friendship that has endured throughout the years

Chapter One

Village of Olgossa
Darfur, Sudan
1877

The birds stopped singing first.

My sister's hand went rigid in mine, her callused fingers, already hardened from grinding grain though she was only eleven, squeezing until my bones ached. I opened my mouth to ask what was wrong, but she pressed her palm across my lips. Her eyes, wide as a gazelle sensing lions, stared past my shoulder into the acacia grove.

Run. The word screamed inside my head. *Drop the firewood. Run.*

But my legs had turned to stone. My sister's grip anchored me to the red earth as surely as the baobab's roots, and even the leaves hung motionless, as if the wind itself held its breath.

Then they came.

Four men on horses exploded from the trees, faces wrapped in indigo cloth that left only their eyes visible, hard and black as beetles. The lead rider's horse bore down on us, foam flying from its mouth, hooves throwing up clods of dirt that stung my bare legs. The smell hit me all at once: sweat-soaked leather, gun oil, and something metallic.

Fear.

My sister screamed my name, the last time I would ever hear it, and yanked her hand from mine. She ran three steps, maybe four, before the rifle butt caught her temple with a sound like a melon splitting. Her body crumpled against the earth.

The scream building in my throat died there. Some animal instinct strangled it before it could escape, and I stood frozen as one of the men dismounted, smooth despite his bulk, and closed the distance between us in three strides.

He spoke words that meant nothing. Arabic, maybe, or one of the northern dialects. When I didn't respond, couldn't respond, his hands, rough as tree bark, seized my wrists. Rope bit into my skin, burning as he wound it tight.

Father will come, I thought wildly. *Uncle is chief. They'll bring spears.*

Another rider yanked me toward his horse and mounted. The rope attached to my wrists jerked tight, and the horse bolted forward. I stumbled behind, my bare feet catching on roots and stones as pain exploded through my toes. I fell, and the rope tore at my wrists as I was dragged, dirt filling my mouth and nose, scraping away skin.

Laughter, dry and cruel, drove out every warm thing I'd ever known: my mother's humming, my father's stories, the song my sister and I had been singing just moments before.

I got my feet under me and stumbled forward in a nightmare run, half-dragged, blood trailing behind us.

I looked back once. Just once.

My sister lay motionless, a small heap of limbs at an angle that shouldn't be possible. Was her chest moving? I couldn't tell through the tears blurring my vision, past the branches already obscuring her.

Then she was gone. The forest closed between us like a door slamming shut.

They didn't stop until the sun balanced on the horizon like a dying ember.

When the lead rider finally reined his horse, I collapsed, my legs simply giving out. The rope held me upright for a moment, suspended between earth and mounted captor, before he cut me free and I fell.

Every part of me screamed. My feet were raw meat, toenails black with blood, skin peeled away to expose tender flesh beneath. My wrists burned where the rope had abraded them to red rawness, and my throat was so dry that swallowing felt like swallowing glass.

"*Kif.*" One of the men thrust a skin at me.

I stared until he made a drinking gesture. Water. My hands shook so violently I could barely grip it, and when I lifted it to my lips, only a trickle emerged—warm, tasting of metal and salt, barely enough to coat my swollen tongue.

I reached for more. A boot caught me in the ribs and sent me sprawling. The man who'd hit me laughed and slung the water skin over his shoulder.

That's all you get. That's all you're worth.

As darkness fell, they tied my hands behind my back and bound my ankles. I lay on my side watching them build a fire, watching them pass the water skin, watching them roast strips of meat whose smell made my stomach twist with hunger fiercer than the pain in my feet.

When they finally threw me a piece, a strip so tough and salty it was more leather than food, I chewed it slowly, making it last, letting the grease coat my cracked lips though each movement split them further.

Above, stars appeared. The same stars that hung over Olgossa, the same stars that had watched my birth, that had guided my people since before memory.

Mother, I thought as I looked up at them. *Can you see these stars? Do you know where I am?*

But the stars gave no answer. They hung cold and distant, witnesses to ten thousand tragedies, indifferent to one more.

I tried to remember my name, whispered it silently, forming the syllables with my broken lips. I felt the shape of it in my mouth, the meaning of it, the way my mother's voice had sounded calling me in from the fields.

Remember, I told myself. *Whatever happens, remember. That name is who you are.*

I didn't know then how they would beat it out of me. How pain and time and the need to become someone else would wear it away like water wearing stone, how one day I would reach for it and find nothing there, just a blank space where my identity used to be.

The slavers' fire burned to embers. Their snores rose and fell. My body ached with a pain so complete it almost stopped being pain and became just the new state of existence.

In that darkness, bound and bleeding and more alone than I'd ever been, I began the long work of forgetting everything I had been.

Twelve days. Or fifteen. Or twenty.

Time stopped meaning anything except the rhythm of walking, resting, walking again. The sun became my enemy, beating down until my lips split and bled, until my tongue swelled thick, until the world wavered like heat rising from sand.

We walked north, I knew that much from the sun's arc, through scrubland that tore at my ankles with thorns, across dry riverbeds whose stones burned through the calluses forming on my ruined feet, past villages where doors slammed shut and mothers pulled children inside rather than witness what we'd become.

On the fourth day, they added me to a coffle.

Twenty-three of us: mostly children, some young women, a few boys not yet old enough to be dangerous. We were roped together neck to neck with hemp that rubbed our skin raw, then wet, then raw again in an endless cycle. The boy behind me, nine or ten, his tribal scars identifying him as Nuer, whimpered constantly, a sound so soft I felt it more than heard it, vibrating through the rope connecting us.

On the seventh day, he stopped whimpering, stopped walking, and simply folded to the ground as if his bones had dissolved.

The guard, the one with a scar pulling his left eye into a permanent squint, walked over without hurry. His shadow fell across the boy's crumpled form, a brief mercy before his boot connected with the child's ribs.

Once. Twice. Three times.

The boy didn't move, didn't cry out. He'd gone beyond the place where pain could reach him.

I wanted to close my eyes, wanted to turn away, but some instinct told me I needed to witness this. Needed to see what awaited those who couldn't continue, needed to let it carve itself into my memory as warning.

The guard pulled out shears, large ones, like those used for cutting through bone, and severed the rope. The boy's body remained where it fell. We walked on, stepping around him, over him, leaving him to the sun and the vultures already circling.

That night, tied in a pen made of thorn bushes, I dreamed of his mother. Wondered if she was still alive, if she'd seen him taken, if she woke each morning and reached for him and found only absence.

Like my mother must be doing. Reaching for me. Finding nothing.

I'm alive, I wanted to tell her across the distance. *I'm still alive.*

But for how long?

We passed through villages where no one looked at us directly. Doors closed with soft thuds that sounded like final judgments, and mothers pulled children back from doorways, their faces showing horror, pity, and relief. Relief that it was us walking in chains and not them.

I had once been one of those children, watching slave coffles pass, never imagining I could become the shadow, the warning, the fate to be avoided.

Food came once daily, mush that tasted of old grain and dirt, sometimes with strips of dried meat so tough and salty they were more leather than flesh. I chewed each bite slowly, not from care, but because my mouth bled when I moved too fast, the open sores at the corners of my lips splitting with every movement.

Water was given in cruel sips, just enough to keep us alive but never enough to stop the thirst that dried our tongues and cracked our lips. Sometimes I tasted metal and wondered if we were drinking diluted blood.

My toenails turned black and separated from their beds, leaving raw half-moons that collected sand and small stones. The bottoms of my feet were worn open, skin gone to expose nerve and blood vessel, each step an exercise in torment.

I no longer knew where I ended and the pain began. We were one thing, pain and I, inseparable and intimate.

On the twelfth day, or perhaps the fifteenth, we crested a low rise of stone and scrub, and I saw it.

The slave market.

A city of canvas and makeshift structures spread across a shallow valley, its tents rippling in the desert wind like the gills of some enormous beast. Smoke rose from countless fires, and the smell hit us—dung, sweat, gunpowder, and underneath it all, the particular stench of human despair concentrated in one place.

The girl roped in front of me, Asha, I'd learned, from the Fur tribe, began to shake. I felt it through the rope, felt her terror as if it were my own.

We were herded to a pen near the market's edge. Water was brought. Not the cruel sips of the march, but enough to truly drink. Food appeared, thin porridge, but warm, almost generous. My stomach, shrunken from days of near-starvation, cramped around it.

"They're fattening us," whispered an older girl beside me, speaking Daju like my people. "Making us look healthier before they trade us."

The pen's gate opened the next morning. A man entered, tall, fat, dressed in robes whose quality spoke of wealth built on misery. His beard was dyed red at the tips, and kohl lined his eyes, making them calculating as they swept over us.

He moved down the line, examining each captive with practiced eyes. He paused at a girl near the front, yanked her to her feet, and made her open her mouth so he could check her teeth.

My turn came.

Rough hands gripped my jaw, forcing my face toward the light. His touch was neither cruel nor kind, just evaluating, the way one might test fruit for ripeness.

He spoke in Arabic to the guards. I'd begun to understand fragments during the march, words repeated often enough to carve themselves into memory.

"Unusual features. Good bone structure. Spirit not yet broken."

His fingers dug into my cheeks, turning my head side to side. His thumb brushed across my cracked lips, then moved to my eyelid, pulling it back to examine the clarity beneath.

I stayed perfectly still, neither resisting nor obeying, having learned that either extreme invited punishment.

"Pretty," he concluded. "Quiet. She'll sell well to the Turkish merchant who arrived yesterday. He likes them young and strong."

He smiled then, showing teeth stained brown from tobacco and kola nut. The smile never reached his eyes.

Turkish merchant. The words meant nothing to me then. I didn't know they marked the beginning of another chapter in my descent, didn't know that worse things awaited than the march, than the hunger, than the rope cutting into my neck.

They called me Bakhita three days later.

I was standing in the pen when one of the guards pointed at me and spoke the word.

"Bakhita. You. Come."

I didn't understand at first, didn't realize he was addressing me. I had a name, my true name, the one my mother gave me, the one that meant something in our language, that connected me to my people's story.

The guard grabbed my arm and yanked me forward. "Bakhita," he repeated, his breath hot and sour in my face. "That's you now. Fortunate one."

He laughed, a sound so empty of feeling it might have come from a corpse.

I was told to smile when shown to potential buyers. I didn't understand the Arabic fully, but I knew what they wanted. When I didn't obey, when my face stayed frozen in the mask I'd made to hide my fear, I was hit in the mouth. My lip split, filling my mouth with the taste of blood.

"Bakhita," the guard said again, wiping his hand on his robe. "Answer when you're called."

It means 'fortunate'. I didn't know that then, but I knew it wasn't meant kindly. It was said with sneers and cruel jokes. I wasn't Bakhita. I was a girl with a different name, a mother's name, a name full of grass and sun and home.

But that name was already slipping away, already being replaced by their word, their label, their claim on everything I was.

I tried to hold onto it, whispered it into the darkness that night, tasted its syllables on my bleeding tongue. But it was like trying to hold water in cupped hands. With each repetition of Bakhita, with each blow for not responding fast enough, my true name became more distant, more like a dream than a memory, more like something that belonged to someone else.

A girl who no longer existed.

They kept us in pens made from thorn bushes and rope. We weren't alone. Boys too young to fight back but old enough to work. Girls valued for their youth and ability to serve. Women who no longer cried, their eyes as dry and empty as wells with no water.

An old man prayed to Allah in a constant whisper, his lips always moving as his fingers worked wooden beads worn smooth by years of devotion. A girl my age sang to herself until her voice broke, a lullaby in a language I didn't recognize, but the melody was universal, the sound mothers make to soothe frightened children.

Some captives were sold to traders going to faraway markets. Some were beaten for breaking rules. Some disappeared completely in the night.

I learned to listen for footsteps, for chains rattling, for the gate opening. I learned to lower my eyes, to make myself small, to go unnoticed when possible.

I learned to forget I was once someone's daughter, someone's sister, a person with rights and worth and a future beyond the next sunrise.

Asha helped me one night when fever from infected wounds made me shake so violently my teeth rattled. She pressed close, sharing her body heat, her thin arms surprisingly strong as she held me steady.

"Don't die," she whispered in Fur-accented Arabic. "If you die, they win."

It was the first kindness anyone had shown me since my capture. The shock of it brought tears. Not from pain this time, but from the reminder that humanity still existed, even here.

"What's your real name?" I asked, my voice cracked and raw.

She was quiet for so long I thought she wouldn't answer. Then: "I don't remember anymore. They took it."

The words settled over me like a burial shroud. *They took it.* Not just forced a new name on her, but actually stole the memory of who she'd been.

Could that happen to me? Could I truly forget?

I whispered my name into the darkness, once, twice, three times, committing it to memory with desperate intensity.

But even as I did, I felt it slipping, like trying to remember a face seen in a dream. The harder I grasped, the faster it faded.

At night, when guards dozed by their fires and other captives slept fitfully, I would stare up at the stars through gaps in the thorn-bush roof. The same stars that shone over Olgossa, the same stars that had watched my birth, that had guided my people for generations.

Mother. Father. Can you see these stars? Do you know where I am? Are you looking for me?

But I knew the truth. We were too far north now, too deep into the trade routes, too thoroughly erased from the world we'd known.

No rescue was coming.

In those first weeks, I lived in my memories during the brief moments before sleep claimed me. I would close my eyes and walk the paths of Olgossa, sit with my mother as she wove baskets, the rhythmic movement of her hands a meditation. I would listen to my father telling stories beneath the baobab tree, his voice deep and certain, and feel my baby brother's weight against my chest, his breath warm and sweet.

I tried to remember my family's faces, to keep them sharp in my mind. But they blurred as days became weeks, as hunger hollowed my cheeks, as fear drained the color from my world. My sister's cries echoed in my sleep, only to vanish by morning like smoke.

I told myself she had escaped, that she'd brought help, that my father and the village men would appear with spears. I told myself lies because lies felt warmer than truth, and the nights were so cold.

But each morning I woke still captive. Still Bakhita. Still alone.

One night, as fever from my wounds made the world waver and bend, she came to me.

A woman in white, walking barefoot across sand that should have burned but seemed not to touch her at all. At first, I thought she was my mother—the way she moved, graceful and unhurried, reminded me of how my mother had moved through our village: confident, purposeful, loved.

But as she drew closer, I saw this woman was different. Taller, her skin paler, though in the strange light I couldn't tell what color it truly was. She wore white robes that somehow remained clean despite the dust, despite the wind that tore at everything else.

Her face was uncovered, beautiful in a way that had nothing to do with features and everything to do with the light radiating from within.

When she looked at me, I felt seen, truly seen, for the first time since my capture.

She knelt beside me on the sand. I tried to speak, to ask who she was, what she wanted, but no words would come.

It didn't matter. She seemed to understand without my speaking.

Her hand reached out, hovering over my shoulder where the whip had landed, where the skin had split and wept clear fluid mixed with blood. She didn't touch the wound. Didn't need to. The warmth from her palm penetrated deeper than any physical touch could reach.

And suddenly I was home.

Not imagining it. Not remembering it. *Living it.*

I sat beside my mother at the grinding stone, my small hands helping hers push the heavy pestle in circles. The morning sun warmed my back, and the smell of grain dust filled my nose. My mother hummed, that particular melody she always chose when she worked, the one that meant everything was well, everyone was safe, the world was ordered and right.

"You are loved," my mother's voice said, though her lips didn't move, though I knew somehow this wasn't really her speaking but the woman in white speaking through her. "You were loved then. You are loved now. You will always be loved."

The scene shifted.

My father, sitting beneath the baobab tree, telling stories to a circle of children. I was there, pressed against his side, feeling the rumble of his voice through his chest. He spoke of the Daju people, of our ancestors, of the kingdoms we came from, of the strength in our blood.

"You are not forgotten," the woman's voice continued. "Your name may be lost, but you are known. Every hair on your head, every mark on your skin, every tear you've cried—all counted, all remembered, all precious."

My sister appeared then, whole, unhurt, her hand in mine as we walked through tall grass, singing our silly song, laughing at nothing and everything the way children do.

"She lives," the woman said, and I didn't know if she meant my sister had survived the kidnapping or if she lived on in some other way, in some other place. But for this moment, she was alive and whole and happy, and that had to be enough.

The warmth from the woman's hand intensified, not painful, but powerful. It poured into me like water into a dry vessel, filling places I didn't know were empty, reaching corners of my soul I'd hidden even from myself.

"What lies ahead will be dark," she said, her voice no longer coming through my memories but speaking directly. "Darker than you can imagine. You will suffer. You will be broken in ways that seem beyond repair."

I wanted to pull away, to refuse this terrible knowledge. But her other hand came to rest on my other shoulder, holding me steady, holding me present.

"But darkness is not the end. The deepest night comes just before dawn. And you, little one, will see the dawn. Not just for yourself, but for many."

I didn't understand. How could I, enslaved and renamed and sold like cattle, bring dawn to anyone?

"Trust," she said simply. "Endure. Remember that you are loved."

She stood then, her white robes settling around her like wings folding. She looked down at me with such tenderness, such fierce protective care, that my heart broke and healed simultaneously.

"I will not leave you," she said. "Even when you cannot see me, cannot feel me, cannot believe I exist. I will not leave you. Never."

Then she was gone, dissolving into light that scattered across the sand like water, like stars, like hope made visible.

I woke gasping, tears streaming down my face, my wounds still burning but somehow more bearable. Asha's hand rested on my shoulder, the same shoulder where the woman had placed hers, warm and real and human.

"You were dreaming," Asha whispered. "You kept saying 'don't leave' over and over."

I couldn't explain what I'd seen, didn't have words for it. But something had changed. Some fundamental shift had occurred in the architecture of my soul.

I was still enslaved. Still called by a name that wasn't mine. Still facing horrors I couldn't imagine.

But I was not alone.

In the days that followed, I whispered into the dark whenever I could. Not words or names, just sounds of longing. A silent prayer to whatever power might listen, might remember the girl I had been, might someday lead me back to myself.

If there was a God, I didn't know His name. But He had heard mine once. I prayed He hadn't forgotten it.

In that name, now as lost to me as my homeland, was everything I had been and might have become: a daughter of Darfur, a child of the Daju, a girl whose future had held marriage and children and the simple dignity of living free under the sun.

Instead, I was Bakhita now. The fortunate one. A cruel joke that would brand me through years of slavery, through owners who would use me, through pain that would have broken someone less stubborn.

But deep inside, in that secret place where not even the cruelest master could reach, I remained unnamed. Waiting. Enduring.

I hadn't been born into silence and shadows. I had been born into song and sunlight.

The stars that watched over the slave pen were the same stars that shone over Olgossa, the same stars that had witnessed my birth and my mother's lullabies and my father's evening prayers. They had watched me play in the tall grass with my sister and had seen the moment the slavers came.

And they would watch what came next.

The woman in white had promised I would see the dawn, that darkness was not the end, that I would endure not just for myself, but for many.

I didn't understand her words then, couldn't imagine how a slave girl with a stolen name could bring light to anyone.

But I held onto them anyway, held them the way I'd once held my sister's hand, with everything I had, knowing they might be torn away but refusing to let go until the very last moment.

The guard's footsteps approached the pen. Keys rattled, and the gate creaked open.

"Bakhita," he called.

I rose slowly, my wounds protesting, and moved toward the sound of my new name.

Behind me, Asha whispered something I didn't catch. Ahead, the guard waited with impatience etched on his face, ready to deliver me to whatever came next.

I took a breath. The air tasted of dust and ash and the faint metallic tang of fear—my own and everyone else's in this pen.

Then I stepped forward into the unknown.

Not as the girl I had been. She was already fading, her name dissolving like salt in water, her future erased like footprints in sand.

But as something else: something harder, something that could bend without breaking completely, something that could carry the woman in white's promise through whatever darkness lay ahead.

I will not leave you, she had said. *Never.*

And somehow, impossibly, in that moment between one step and the next, I believed her.

The long road stretched before me. A road that would lead through hell before finding its way toward something like freedom.

But I would walk it.

I would survive.

And one day, though I couldn't yet see how or when, I would speak. Not to reclaim my original name, for that was lost forever, but to tell this story, to bear witness to the darkness and the light, to become a voice for all the nameless ones who would never have the chance to speak for themselves.

The guard grabbed my arm and pulled me from the pen.

The gate slammed shut behind me.

And the journey continued.

Chapter Two

They chained us before the sun rose—twenty-three of us, neck to iron neck. The slavers worked quickly in the darkness, their hands practiced, efficient. Metal bit into my throat. Would bite for the next six hundred miles, though I didn't know that yet. I didn't know that seven of us would never see El-Obeid.

"Move!" The lead slaver cracked his whip above our heads. "North. No stopping."

Darkness still gripped the earth. The night animals had fallen silent, waiting. My bare feet found the first steps on sand that would shred them to raw meat before this journey ended.

The boy chained behind me was younger than my brother Kishmet, maybe six harvests old. I felt him trembling through the chain links. Three small tugs. Pause. Three more.

I didn't know if he was trying to tell me something or simply shaking with fear. I tugged back once. Gently. *I'm here.*

His trembling steadied. Just slightly.

It was the last kindness I would offer for days.

The chains allowed no mercy. When the girl ahead of me stumbled, the iron yanked my neck forward. When I slowed, it choked the boy behind me. We learned quickly. Match pace or strangle.

By midday, the sun had become our true master. It pulled water from my body, turned my tongue to leather, split my lips. I tasted blood when I tried to swallow.

But I also tasted something else. A memory of my sister Kishmet and me stealing honey from the clay pot my mother kept for feast days. The sweetness coating our fingers, our guilty laughter, the way the sunlight had streamed through our hut's doorway turning everything golden.

I held that memory in my mouth like water. Let it dissolve slowly.

They gave us water at noon. One guard held a skin, another his rifle.

"Drink fast." The guard tipped the skin. Warm, iron-tasting liquid splashed my mouth. Three swallows. Four. Then he yanked it away.

The water vanished down my throat, waking thirst worse than before. My body screamed for more. The guard had already moved to the next captive.

I learned then: small mercies make torture sharper.

As the sun climbed higher, a bird crossed the sky. Just one. A hornbill with its distinctive curved beak, flying south. Flying toward the grasslands. Flying home.

I watched it until it disappeared, a black speck against endless blue.

The boy behind me made a small sound. Not quite a sob. Something caught between grief and wonder, as though he too had seen the bird and remembered there was a world beyond chains.

They chained me to a Fur girl on the next day. Scars marked her cheeks—three parallel lines that told me she'd been old enough for the cutting ceremony before she was taken. Older than me. Maybe twelve harvests.

Her name was Asha. I knew because she whispered it once, just once, when they first locked us together.

"Bakhita," I whispered back. The name they'd given me. Not my real name. Never my real name.

Her lips moved silently. I read them in the moonlight that first night: *What was your real name?*

I shook my head. Couldn't speak it aloud. If I said it, I would shatter.

She nodded. Understanding without explanation—the language of the stolen.

Her wrists had been rubbed raw. The iron had stripped away skin, left meat exposed. Clear fluid leaked from the wounds, mixed with blood. Flies gathered there. She'd stopped brushing them away.

But her eyes stayed alert. Sharp. She watched the guards, counted their rotations, noted which ones fell asleep first after evening prayers.

She was planning something. Escape or death, I couldn't tell which.

We didn't speak after that first night. Breath cost too much. Instead, we learned the chain's language. One sharp tug meant danger, a guard approaching, a snake on the path. A gentle pull offered encouragement. A rhythmic sway said *I see you. You're not alone.*

This became our conversation. A dialogue of tension and release through iron links.

On the morning of the third day, I felt Asha's steps grow uncertain. The chain slackened, then jerked tight. Slackened again. Her breathing had changed—shallow, rapid, urgent.

"Keep moving!" A guard's voice behind us.

Asha's legs folded. One moment she walked; the next, she knelt in the sand as though someone had cut her strings. The chain yanked me down beside her. My knees cracked against stone hidden beneath the surface.

We knelt there together, her breath coming in gasps, mine frozen in my throat.

She looked at me. Her eyes were clear. Fully present. Not clouded with pain or fear.

She'd chosen this moment. This was her escape.

"Thank you," she mouthed.

The scarred guard approached. I knew him by the puckered flesh that pulled his left eye into a permanent sneer. His shadow fell across us, the only cool thing for miles.

His boot connected with Asha's ribs.

Crack.

Like dry acacia wood breaking. Like a clay pot struck with stone. That sound would echo in my dreams for years.

Asha didn't cry out. She held my gaze, and something passed between us. Recognition. Release. Blessing.

He struck her again with his rifle butt. Wood against skull. The second blow left a hollow at her temple, a depression that shouldn't exist in living bone.

"Please." The word escaped my mouth before I could stop it.

The guard's eyes found mine. "You want to join her?"

I wanted to say yes. Wanted to kneel beside her and let the rifle butt find my skull too. Wanted this journey to end.

But Asha's eyes were still on me. *Live,* they said. *Someone has to remember.*

I dropped my gaze to the sand. Watched my tears make dark circles in the dust.

Metal shrieked as he cut the chain between us. Two snips with bolt cutters. The weight lifted from my neck, Asha's weight, Asha's life.

He yanked me to my feet, shoved me toward the line stumbling ahead. I walked. The iron around my throat felt lighter now, obscene in its lightness.

Behind me, Asha lay twisted in the sand. Her mouth had stopped moving. Her eyes stared at the sky, finally seeing something beyond this world.

I didn't look back. But I carried her with me. Her courage. Her choice. Her final gift.

That night, she walked beside me in dreams. Not a ghost. A companion. Telling me stories in the language of the Fur people, words I didn't understand but found comforting nonetheless.

We camped in a dry riverbed where ancient waters had once flowed. The curved banks still held the memory of rain, though none had fallen in years. Guards drank fermented mare's milk around their fire, laughed at jokes I didn't understand. Their voices carried across the darkness, harsh, alive, human.

I sat with my knees pulled to my chest, shivering despite the warm wind. Around me, the others had collapsed into sleep or something like it,that exhausted state beyond crying, beyond feeling.

The moon was three-quarters full. My mother would have called it the Planting Moon, time to put millet seeds in the ground. Was she looking at this same moon? Did she wonder if I saw it too?

Mama.

The word rose from somewhere deep inside me. Not formed in words, not directed at anyone. Just longing flung upward toward whatever might receive it.

Mama, mama, mama.

I must have slept. Because she came.

At first, I thought it was my mother. Same height, same way of moving with her hips leading, her shoulders back. But as she drew closer, I saw the white robe, unstained by dust. Saw her feet, bare like mine, but uncut, the soles smooth as river stones.

The woman walked across the sand as though it were soft grass. Each step she took left no print, the grains falling back into place behind her as if she weighed nothing at all.

Wind that had scoured my skin raw parted around her like water around a stone. The night air carried her scent: frankincense and something else. Something like the smell of rain about to fall, that green-wet promise that makes the earth hold its breath.

Light spilled from beneath her veil. Not the harsh white of the moon, but golden. Honey-colored. The exact shade of sunlight through my mother's doorway on that last morning before the raiders came.

I should have been afraid. Instead, I reached for her with my chained hands.

She knelt beside me. The movement was liquid, effortless. Her knees made no sound touching the sand.

Up close, I couldn't see her face. The veil remained in place. But I felt her gaze on me. Not evaluating like the slavers, not pitying like the villagers. Seeing. Truly seeing. Every part of me that remained beneath the bruises and blood.

Her hand lifted toward my shoulder where the whip had landed that morning. Where skin had split and now wept clear fluid mixed with blood. I flinched without meaning to.

She paused. Waited.

I made myself stay still.

Her palm settled on the wound. The touch burned with presence, not pain. Heat that wasn't temperature. Pressure that wasn't weight.

Her fingers pressed against something deeper than flesh. Touched the place where memory lived.

Suddenly I stood in my mother's kitchen. Not remembering it. *Standing* there. The cooking fire crackled, sending sparks spiraling upward through the smoke hole. The smell of millet porridge bubbled in the clay pot, thick and nutty and real. My mother's voice hummed that wordless tune she always sang while grinding grain, the rhythm matching the circular motion of her arms.

She turned. Saw me.

"*Daughter.*"

My real name. The name I couldn't speak aloud anymore, she said it. The syllables fell on me like cool water, like shade after burning sun, like arms that would hold me forever.

I ran to her. Felt her arms close around me—strong, safe, *home*. Felt her chin rest on top of my head the way it always did. Felt her heartbeat against my ear, steady as drums at the harvest dance.

"I'm here, little one. I'm here."

Real. Complete. Whole.

Then it shattered.

I woke with tears cutting clean tracks through the dust on my face. My throat ached from swallowing sobs in sleep. My shoulder where the woman had touched me felt warm, the pain somehow distant.

The woman had gone, if she'd ever been there outside my desperate mind.

But the wound on my shoulder had closed. Not healed, I would carry that scar forever. But the bleeding had stopped. The edges had knitted together impossibly fast, skin meeting skin.

And something else remained. Some presence lingering just beyond sight. A sense that I had been *seen* by a power that knew my real name, even though I could no longer speak it.

Not hope. Hope was too bright, too bold for this place.

But perhaps hope's seed. A crack in the wall of despair, hairline-thin, through which light might eventually grow.

I found my thoughts reaching toward that presence as we marched. My mind stretched for it the way desert grasses lean toward water they sense underground, roots seeking what eyes cannot see.

I had no words for prayer. The old gods of my people dealt with rain and harvest, with cattle fertility and crop abundance. They weren't gods you talked to, but gods you appeased with offerings.

But this presence, however, felt different. It felt like it might listen.

So, I tried. Wordless, shapeless, just pain thrown upward like a stone into a well, waiting to hear if it reached bottom or kept falling forever.

Are you there?

Can you see me?

Do I matter to you?

No answer came. But the act of asking changed something inside me. Created space where before there had been only choking despair.

Ahead of me, the old man collapsed.

He'd been praying since the first day, his lips always moving, his fingers working wooden beads worn smooth by years of touch. The beads were dark acacia wood, each one carved with symbols I didn't recognize. Muslim prayers, maybe. Or something older.

The guards had let him pray, superstition, maybe, or simple indifference to what didn't slow the march.

But on day eight, his legs simply stopped. He folded onto the sand with dignity, still clutching his prayer beads, his lips still forming words.

The guards gathered around him. Their shadows fell across his body like vultures circling.

I closed my eyes. Heard the discussion—whether to waste a bullet, whether he was worth the effort.

"Leave him. He'll be dead before nightfall."

When they pushed us forward, I looked back once.

The old man lay on his side, curled like a child sleeping. His fingers still worked the beads. His mouth still moved, shaping prayers with his last breaths.

But here's what I remember most: he was smiling. Faint, barely visible. But unmistakable.

His faith hadn't protected his body. His lifetime of prayers hadn't earned him mercy from the slavers.

But something on his face showed peace. As though his prayers were being answered in ways invisible to the rest of us. As though someone had come to walk him home.

I hoped so. Hoped he died with company rather than alone. Hoped that whatever power he'd spent his life addressing had finally answered.

When I looked forward again, I found my own lips moving. No words. No language. Just shapes forming silently, mimicking the old man's devotion.

If faith could bring that kind of peace at the end, maybe it was worth cultivating. Even here. Especially here.

My toenails had turned black. One by one, they separated from their beds, leaving raw half-moons that collected sand and stones. The soles of my feet had worn through, skin gone, nerve exposed, each step an act of will.

I no longer knew where I ended and the pain began. We had merged, pain and I. Become one thing, inseparable.

But I learned something: pain could be befriended. Not conquered. Not ignored. But acknowledged. *You're here. I feel you. But you're not all of me.*

Every step became a kind of prayer. Each placement of ruined foot on burning sand. Each adjustment of shoulders under the chain's weight. All of it ritual. All of it defiance.

I'm still here.

You haven't erased me.

I remember my name even if I can't speak it.

We passed through a village at midday. Doors closed with soft thuds. Final judgments made without words. Mothers pulled their children back from doorways, their faces showing horror, pity, relief.

Thank the gods it's not us.

I had once been one of those children. Watching through cracks in walls, hoping the shadows would pass by.

Now I was the shadow. The warning. The terrible example.

But as we walked through that village, I made myself look at each closed door, remember each face I glimpsed before shutters slammed. Made myself real to them, even if they wanted to forget.

One small girl, maybe four harvests old, escaped her mother's grip. She ran to the edge of the path and held out a mango, overripe, already browning on one side.

"Here," she said. Her voice high, uncertain. "Are you hungry?"

Her mother snatched her back with a cry. The mango fell in the dust.

A guard kicked it aside, laughing.

But I saw it. That small girl, offering what little she had. Seeing us as human rather than shadow.

I tucked that moment inside me next to the honey-stealing memory, next to Asha's final gift, next to my mother's arms. Building a collection of light to carry into darkness.

At sunset, we climbed a low ridge of stone and scrub.

Beyond it stretched a sight that stopped even our captors: a city of tents and makeshift structures spread across a shallow valley. Canvas walls rippled in the wind like the gills of fish gasping for air. Fires dotted the camp, their smoke rising in columns against the darkening sky.

Sounds carried across the distance. Shouts in Arabic and languages I didn't know. Camels braying. Metal striking metal. Occasional laughter that sounded wrong in this place.

The air reeked. Dung, sweat, gunpowder, human waste. A stench so powerful that several of the younger children vomited, nothing but bile from empty stomachs.

We had arrived at El-Obeid. The slave market.

The boy behind me, the one who'd trembled that first morning, made a sound in his throat. Not fear. Resignation. The sound of someone who'd hoped against hope for rescue and now understood none would come.

I tugged the chain gently. One pull. *I'm still here.*

No answer. He'd gone somewhere inside himself. Somewhere I couldn't follow.

A man stood at the camp's entrance. Tall and fat. His robes were fine cotton, dyed deep indigo, the color of wealth. His beard had been hennaed red at the tips. Kohl lined his eyes, emphasizing their calculating coldness.

He examined us as we approached. Ran his gaze along backs, hips, legs. Noted height, muscle, potential. His expression never changed from pure evaluation, like a farmer examining cattle.

When he reached me, he stopped.

"This one. Bring her here."

The guard shoved me forward. The man's fingers, callused, impersonal, gripped my jaw. Turned my face toward the dying light.

"Unusual," he said in Arabic. I'd begun to understand the language, words seeping into understanding through repetition. "Nilotic features. Good bone structure. Strong despite the journey."

His thumb pressed against my split lips. I tasted salt from his skin, bitter and human.

He pulled my eyelid back to examine the white beneath. Pried open my mouth to check my teeth. Squeezed my arm to test muscle.

I held perfectly still. Neither resisting nor obeying. I'd learned that either extreme invited punishment.

But inside, I was cataloging. *His breath smells of coffee. His hands have a scar across the knuckles, old, raised. He favors his left leg slightly.*

Small details. Small rebellions. Proof I still observed. Still thought. Still existed as more than merchandise.

"Pretty." He smiled. Brown-stained teeth from tobacco and kola nut. The smile never touched his eyes. "Quiet. But I see unbroken spirit in those eyes. The Turkish merchant will pay well for this one."

He released my face, gestured to his assistant.

"Clean her up. Treat the worst wounds. Present her tomorrow when Rahmani arrives. She's premium goods."

Premium goods. As though I were bolts of cloth or sacks of grain.

But beneath my carefully blank expression, something stirred. The presence I'd felt since the woman in white had touched me. The wordless prayer I'd been forming. The collection of light-moments I'd gathered.

They could name me Bakhita. Could chain my body. Could sell me like grain.

But they couldn't touch the space inside me where my real name lived. Where my mother's voice still hummed. Where Asha's courage and the old man's peace and the small girl's mango all resided, luminous and real.

The guards pushed us into the market. Its noise swallowed us—haggling voices, crying children, the clink of coins changing hands.

The sun had set completely now. Stars emerged, cold and distant. But I looked up anyway, found the constellation my father had shown me, the Water Bearer, pouring life onto the earth.

"That one never moves," he'd said. "No matter how lost you get, you can always find home by those stars."

I couldn't find home and would never see my family again.

This knowledge settled with the weight of absolute certainty. What lay ahead was not freedom but deeper slavery. Not salvation but further degradation.

Yet even as they herded us toward the holding pens, that wordless prayer continued to pulse within me. A counterpoint to the rhythm of my destroyed feet on sand.

I had survived fifteen days. Seven others had not.

I was Bakhita now, 'the fortunate one'. The cruelest joke, a name that mocked with every use.

But beneath that forced identity, behind the mask of submission I wore like armor, something persistent remained.

The woman in white had seen it. Had touched the wound it lived in and made it real.

I was more than merchandise. More than a slave. More than fear and pain and loss.

I was someone whose real name was spoken with love in my mother's kitchen. Someone who'd shared honey-stealing laughter with her sister. Someone Asha had trusted with her last moments. Someone the old man's faith walked alongside. Someone a small girl had seen as worthy of her only mango.

I was a collection of light carried into darkness.

They could sell my body. But they couldn't purchase what made me human.

I stepped into the slave market holding this truth like a candle cupped in my palms.

The nightmare's next chapter was beginning.

But so was something else. Something I was learning to name.

Resistance. Not the kind that breaks chains.

The kind that remembers.

Chapter Three

They brought me into the courtyard at dawn.

The sky was still dark, stars fading. I had been in Khadija's household for three weeks now, long enough to learn the rhythms of the women's quarters, the particular cruelties of my new mistress, but not long enough to anticipate what awaited me.

I had arrived in Khartoum a month earlier, sold for the third time since my capture. My new master was a wealthy Turkish merchant who traded in ivory and indigo, and whose compound sprawled along the bank where the Blue and White Nile met. The city rose from the desert like a fever dream—mud brick buildings beside structures of stone, minarets calling the faithful to prayer, boats with triangular sails carrying cargo up and down the river. I saw little of it. I was taken directly to the women's quarters, a separate building where my master's wives and female slaves lived apart from the men.

There I met Khadija.

She was my master's second wife, about forty years old, with features that might once have been beautiful but had hardened into permanent dissatisfaction. The other slaves called her Al-Sayida, the Lady, their voices dropping to whispers when they spoke of her.

"This is the new one?" she had asked that first day, her eyes sliding over me as one examines livestock. "She is thin. Ugly. What did my husband pay for this scarecrow?"

I was given various duties—carrying water from the courtyard well, washing clothes in the stone basins, sweeping the tiled floors, helping prepare meals in the kitchen where the air was thick with cumin and coriander. I learned quickly. A broken dish meant a beating with a thin rod that raised welts but left no permanent marks. Spilled water meant no food for a day. Every mistake carried its own precise punishment.

But these everyday cruelties were just the beginning.

Three weeks into my service, I was called to Khadija's chamber before dawn. This was unusual. My duties typically began after the morning call to prayer, and I approached with dread, uncertain what wrong I might have committed.

The room was arranged differently than I had seen it before. The usual furniture had been pushed to the walls, leaving an open space in the center. A low wooden table stood there, its surface covered with objects that gleamed in the lamplight—knives of various sizes, small brass pots, bundles of herbs, bottles of dark liquid.

Khadija was not alone. Three women were with her. Older women with hands stained dark from years of working with dyes and pigments, their faces expressionless as ancient statues. They wore clothes unlike any I had seen in the household, decorated with protective charms and cowrie shells that clicked softly when they moved.

"Remove your clothing," Khadija instructed.

I hesitated, confusion temporarily overcoming obedience.

"Remove it," she repeated, her voice hardening, "or it will be removed for you."

I obeyed, my fingers fumbling with the simple ties of my shirt, acutely aware of the five pairs of eyes on my exposed skin. I had not been naked before others since the slave markets, and vulnerability sent a tremor through my body I could not control.

"Lie down," one of the older women said, pointing to the table. "On your stomach first."

The wood was cold against my skin. I turned my head to one side, my cheek pressed against the surface, and saw Khadija watching with an expression that sent ice through my veins.

"She is unmarked," one woman observed, running a rough hand along my back. "A blank canvas. Rare, in one her age."

"That is why I selected her," Khadija replied. "The others had tribal markings already. I wanted one untouched, suitable for the designs I have planned."

"It will take time," another woman cautioned. "The pattern you've shown us is extensive. There will be risk of fever, of infection."

"Begin," Khadija said. "We have until midday."

I heard the conversation in fragments, unable to piece together its full meaning. Then I felt hands positioning me more precisely on the table, adjusting my limbs to expose my back, my shoulders, my thighs. I heard the clink of metal against ceramic, soft murmurs in a dialect I did not fully understand.

And then I felt the first cut.

The knife was sharp, its blade heated to seal the wound even as it carved. The pain was unlike anything I had known—precise, intimate, deliberate. Not the blunt hurt of a beating or the dull ache of hunger, but an exquisite agony that claimed my complete attention, that allowed no retreat into the disconnected state that had become my refuge.

I did not scream at first. Pride or shock held my voice captive as the knife traced its initial pattern across my shoulder blade—a curved line that branched into smaller arcs, a design whose meaning I could not see but whose burning passage I felt with terrible clarity.

The second cut followed the first, intersecting it, extending the pattern down my spine. The third traced a matching line on my opposite shoulder. By the fourth cut, a sound escaped me—not a scream but a whimper, thin and high.

"She will need to be held," one of the women stated. "They always struggle eventually."

Hands pressed down on my wrists, on my ankles, on the small of my back, gentle but unstoppable. The cutting continued, each incision adding to the map of pain spreading across my skin.

After the twelfth cut, I drifted away.

My mind, unable to contain such concentrated suffering, separated from my body. Not entirely, the pain remained a howling presence, but partially, creating a strange doubling. Part of me remained on the table, every nerve screaming. But another part floated somewhere near the ceiling, watching the scene with detachment.

I saw myself from above. A thin, dark girl spread out on a wooden table, blood tracing patterns across her skin. I saw the women bent over their work, foreheads creased with concentration. I saw Khadija watching, her eyes bright with satisfaction that seemed to go beyond the aesthetic.

From this divided state, I witnessed the continuation of my mutilation as if it were happening to someone else, a girl I knew intimately but was not, quite, identical with.

Time lost its ordinary quality. The cutting seemed to exist in an eternal present, neither beginning nor ending but simply being. I heard voices as if underwater, muffled, distorted, occasionally penetrating my haze.

"The symmetry must be perfect."

"Pass the salt mixture."

"Hold her leg still. This pattern requires absolute precision."

"How many cuts so far?"

"Eighty-seven."

The number cut through my disconnection, anchoring me momentarily to physical reality. Eighty-seven incisions, and more to come. I tried to count them, to focus on numbers rather than pain, but kept losing track, my mind slipping away like a boat untied from its mooring.

When they turned me over to begin work on my chest and stomach, fresh shame cut through the haze. A different pain, emotional rather than physical, yet no less acute. I closed my eyes, unable to bear the sight of faces hovering above me, of hands holding blades that would continue their inexorable redesign of the body I inhabited.

The cutting resumed. New patterns, new pathways of fire across my flesh. The salt mixture they rubbed into the wounds burned with an intensity that made the initial cutting seem almost gentle, a secondary agony designed to ensure the scars would rise and remain permanent, visible testament to the artistry inflicted upon me.

Through it all, Khadija watched. Sometimes she approached the table, examining the progress with critical attention, suggesting adjustments to the design. Sometimes she reclined on her cushions, sipping tea as if attending a performance. Her presence became more terrible than the knives themselves, the driving will behind the suffering.

"One hundred and fourteen," a voice announced finally. "It is complete."

I felt hands applying paste to the cuts: something cool and astringent that momentarily dulled the burning. Cloths were wrapped around my torso, my thighs, my arms. The pressure of the bandages brought fresh waves of pain, duller now, more generalized.

"Take her to the small room behind the kitchen," Khadija instructed. "Keep her isolated until the initial healing is complete. We don't want infection spreading to the other slaves."

I was lifted from the table, my body unresponsive to my own commands, and carried through corridors that seemed to stretch and contract. The small room was little more than a closet, windowless and bare except for a thin pallet. I was placed there with surprising gentleness, a blanket draped over me despite the heat.

"Drink this," one woman said, holding a cup to my lips. The liquid was bitter, medicinal, but I swallowed obediently. Almost immediately, heaviness spread through my limbs, darkness at the edges of my vision.

"It will help her sleep through the worst of it," I heard the woman explain. "Give her water when she wakes, but no food until tomorrow. And change the bandages when they become soaked through."

Darkness claimed me then, not the velvet darkness of natural sleep but something deeper and more absolute.

I emerged from this artificial night in fragments. I was aware first of thirst, a dry desolation that made even breathing painful. Then of heat, my skin burning with fever. Then of hands—cool cloths pressed against my forehead, liquid dribbled between cracked lips, bandages removed and replaced with murmured words.

Time passed unmarked. Days, perhaps. The fever rose and fell like tides, carrying me into delirium and then retreating, leaving me exhausted but clear-headed in its wake. During these periods of clarity, I began to reassemble myself, to gather the scattered fragments and press them back together.

I was Bakhita. I had been taken from my home. I had walked the desert in chains. I had been sold three times. I had been cut one hundred and fourteen times to satisfy the vanity of a woman who saw in me not a person but a possession to be altered according to her whims.

I repeated these facts to myself, a litany that helped me hold onto myself when fever and pain tried to wash me away. But as I rebuilt this narrative, I noticed something fundamental had changed.

The split that occurred during the cutting had not fully healed. Part of me now watched my body from a distance, as if I stood slightly outside myself. This separation created a gap between what happened to me and how much I suffered from it. The gap helped me survive what might otherwise have broken me. But it also changed something essential.

My thoughts came in fragments now, in broken pieces that reflected the splintering of my consciousness. Sometimes I spoke of myself as "I," claiming ownership of my experiences. But increasingly, I found myself thinking of "she," of "the girl," of "Bakhita" as if observing another being whose fate was linked to mine but whose suffering I could regard with detachment.

"She feels thirst," I whispered once to the slave woman who tended me. "Her lips are dry."

The woman looked at me strangely but brought water nonetheless.

As the initial healing progressed and the fever receded, I was allowed to rise from my pallet, to take tentative steps, to accustom myself to standing again. The bandages were removed, revealing what had been done—a map of raised welts circling my torso, my thighs, my arms. Geometric patterns in the Bedouin style mixed with stylized flowers and abstract symbols whose meaning remained opaque to me.

I could not see my back, but I could feel it. Ridges of scar tissue that pulled uncomfortably with certain movements, that would remain sensitive for years to come.

The woman who had performed the cutting returned once to inspect her handiwork, nodding with professional satisfaction.

"The design has taken well," she informed Khadija. "The scarring is clean, raised but not excessive. The patterns are clear and will remain visible as the girl ages."

Khadija circled me, her gaze critical yet pleased. "Yes. It is as I envisioned. She is transformed."

I stood motionless under this inspection, my eyes focused on a point beyond the room, beyond the walls. The part of me that observed from a distance noted how the girl called Bakhita had learned to absent herself even while physically present, how her consciousness could slip away like water between stones.

"When can she resume her duties?" Khadija asked.

"Another week for final healing," came the reply. "But she can begin light work tomorrow. The movement will prevent the scars from tightening too severely."

And so, I returned to the life I had known before, carrying water, sweeping floors, preparing food, but I returned changed. The girl who had been brought to the courtyard at dawn now existed in fragments: one that moved through the world, performing tasks, avoiding punishment, surviving; and another that watched from somewhere just behind the eyes, recording experiences without fully inhabiting them.

In the days that followed, I became an object of curiosity within the household. Other slaves regarded me with a mixture of pity and awe, keeping their distance. Visitors to the women's quarters would sometimes ask to see "the marked one," and I would be called to display the artistry carved into my flesh, required to stand still while strange hands traced the patterns without regard for the person who bore them.

Khadija enjoyed these displays, accepting compliments as if she herself had wielded the knives. I came to understand that I served as demonstration of both her wealth, for the procedure had been costly, and her power, her ability to impose her aesthetic upon the very body of another being.

I learned that I was not the first to be so marked. Two other slave girls bore smaller patterns on their shoulders or backs. They spoke to me sometimes of their experiences, offering salves to ease the persistent itching of healing scars.

"You survived," one told me, her voice low as we worked together sorting lentils in the kitchen. "That is what matters. The cuts heal. Even the memory of pain fades, eventually."

"Does it?" I asked, genuinely curious.

She considered this, her hands continuing their mechanical sorting. "Not entirely. But it changes form. Becomes less immediate. More like a story you know than a thing you felt."

A story. Not happening now, but recorded. Remembered.

That night, as I lay on my pallet in the small room that had become mine, a small privacy granted perhaps because I was now a valuable investment, I tried to gather the scattered pieces of myself.

"I am Bakhita," I whispered into the darkness. "I was taken from my home. I was marked against my will. I endure."

The words dissolved before I could hold them. Bakhita. That name belonged to the body on this mat, the skin that still burned and itched. But the part of me that spoke, that watched, remained nameless, separate, safer.

I was the girl from Olgossa, whose true name had been stolen along with her freedom. I was the physical being who bore one hundred and fourteen decorative scars. And I was the observer who watched from a slight distance, recording the ongoing story of this captive existence.

In dreams that night, I sometimes walked the paths of Olgossa again, whole and unmarked. Sometimes I floated above the Khartoum compound, watching the girl called Bakhita move through her constrained world. And sometimes I stood in a vast emptiness, neither home nor captivity, where past and present existed simultaneously.

From this fragmented state, I woke each morning to face another day. My body grew efficient at its tasks while my mind remained partly elsewhere—present enough to avoid punishment, distant enough to preserve some small flame of self.

The cutting had not killed me, but it had transformed me. I had become multiple pieces in order to remain whole at the core, had to break apart so I would not be entirely destroyed.

I did not know then whether this fracturing was survival or surrender, victory or defeat. I knew only that the girl called Bakhita continued. Kept living. Kept watching. Kept remembering.

And somewhere, in the spaces between these fragments, something waited. Patient, watchful, neither completely broken nor completely whole. Something becoming.

What shape it would eventually take, what name it might claim, I could not yet imagine. For now, it was enough that it endured, like a seed hidden beneath the scarred surface of a life forever altered by what happened in the marking room.

A seed that might, against all odds, one day find light.

Chapter Four

I lost count of the days, then the seasons, then the years.

I was passed from one master to another. Each household spoke a different dialect, but cruelty needed no translation. My body learned to obey before my ears understood the command.

In the years between the marking and my arrival in the house with white walls, I passed through three more households. A Turkish officer who kept his slaves in shuttered rooms. A merchant who traded me for less than the cost of a brass bowl. Each taught me the same lesson in different languages: I was property, nothing more. But it was in El-Obeid, in the house of an Arab merchant whose name I am still afraid to say, that something inside me finally broke.

His wealth showed in everything—brass lamps casting intricate shadows, carpets so thick footsteps made no sound, fountains running ceaselessly in the courtyard despite the desert sun. His daughters, with henna-stained fingers and kohl-lined eyes, required little of me at first. I brushed their hair until it shone, fastened their gold anklets, stood silent as another shadow when they received visitors.

By night, I slept in a narrow alcove beside their chambers, where the air hung thick with jasmine and ambergris. The moon cast latticed patterns across my skin that resembled the scars I already bore. I traced them with my fingertips, remembering who I had been before I became merely an extension of another's will.

The elder daughter sometimes called me to read poetry aloud, though she knew I could not decipher the elegant script. It amused her to hear me stumble over words I did not understand. The younger one, still a child, would sometimes leave pomegranate seeds beside my sleeping mat, small rubies of kindness I dared not acknowledge.

Then the merchant's son returned from a journey.

The household shifted in his presence. Servants moved with downcast eyes. Even the fountain seemed to murmur more quietly. I was arranging cushions in the women's quarters when he entered, his shadow preceding him.

"You," he said. "Fetch wine."

I moved to obey, but in my haste, I stumbled against a small table of inlaid mother-of-pearl. An inkwell toppled. Darkness spread across the scroll he had placed there, devouring words I could not read.

The silence lasted three heartbeats.

Then his hand struck my face, knocking me sideways into the wall.

"Do you know what you have destroyed?" His voice was quiet. Worse than shouting.

I prostrated myself; forehead pressed against the floor, and waited.

The whip came first. I heard it whistle through air before it tore into my shoulders. The second stroke fell before I could draw breath. By the third, the room had narrowed to a point of white light surrounded by darkness.

I cannot recall how many times the leather fell. Memory has drawn a veil across the precise count. What remains is the moment his boots entered my field of vision—fine tooled leather, immaculate except for a single drop of my blood like a crimson star upon the toe.

He kicked me then. Not wildly, but with precision.

My ribs first. Each impact a dull thunder through bone. When I could no longer raise my arms to shield myself, he turned to my legs, methodically ensuring no part of me would be spared.

I stopped counting after the seventh blow. The body can only hold so much before it lets go.

Mine let go.

When consciousness began to slip away, I heard rather than saw him leave. The rustle of his robes. The measured tread of his steps. The closing of the door. Each sound echoing in the space where thought should have been.

Hours later, or perhaps only moments, the younger daughter found me. Her gasp pierced the haze. Cool hands touched my brow. Rapid words were exchanged. I felt myself being moved, though I could not help.

They placed me in a storeroom where olives and grain were kept. The air was dense with fermentation. Light filtered through a high, narrow opening, casting a single blade of brightness that traveled slowly across the earthen floor as days passed into nights and back again.

I lay there, a heap of broken flesh. My body became a landscape of pain I traversed without moving. Fever came, a red tide that swept me far from reason. In delirium, I spoke with ghosts—my mother, whose face had begun to fade; children I had played with in a village whose name I was forgetting; the hyena I had once seen at the edge of firelight, its eyes reflecting flames.

A slave girl brought water, tipping it carefully between my cracked lips. Sometimes the younger daughter appeared to place a cool cloth on my brow or leave bread beside my head. These kindnesses were administered in silence, as if sound might shatter the fragile spell keeping death at bay.

For more than a month, I dwelled in that space between existence and oblivion. The straw beneath me grew foul. Insects explored the topography of my wounds. I watched them with detached curiosity, envying their freedom to come and go.

When I finally could rise—first to my knees, then shakily to my feet—I knew something fundamental had changed. Not just my body, which now bore new scars layered over old, but something deeper. A door had closed inside me. Behind it, I placed all hope that those in power might show mercy, all belief that goodness might be rewarded, all faith that my suffering had meaning.

I returned to my duties like a ghost returning to haunt familiar rooms. The son had left again, but his violence lingered in corners like smoke. The daughters looked at me with pity, but not enough to intercede. The master passed me in hallways without seeing me, as one might pass a piece of furniture too familiar to notice.

And I, who had once possessed a name, a home, a self, moved through my days going through the motions, fetching, carrying, bowing, serving. But beneath my obedience, something cold and watchful had awakened. It measured the depths of my degradation and found them bottomless. It noted every casual cruelty, every careless blow.

This thing inside me waited, as I waited. For what, I did not know. Rescue? Death? Some understanding that might make sense of the cruelty that had become my existence?

I understood then that my suffering was not unique. I was simply one more shadow among countless others, cast by the harsh light of other people's power. Yet even shadows, I thought as sleep finally came, even shadows move when the light shifts. Even shadows might, given time, grow long enough to touch the ones who cast them.

The Turkish officer's wife who owned me next used her cane as one might use a finger, idly, with practiced ease. It landed across our hands, our backs, our feet with the precise indifference of rainfall. I still carry the mark on my forearm where she burned me for breaking a water jug, a constellation of raised flesh, pink and puckered.

She hated my silence.

"You look like a ghost," she hissed once, her breath smelling of cardamom. "Do you not even cry anymore?"

I did not answer. I had forgotten how to cry.

Words flew about me like stones, sharp things that bruised without breaking skin. My tongue sat useless in my mouth, curled against teeth that would not part. Language became my first betrayer. My silence, my only ally.

The other servants called me *spirito muto,* the mute spirit. I preferred that to the name they had given me, a sound that sat on their tongues like something rotten.

"This one is obedient," the officer told a visitor once, his hand heavy on my shoulder. "Worth twice what I paid."

Obedience. That was the word they used for the mask I wore. They did not see what lived behind it—the calculations, the survival, the stubborn ember that refused to dim. My silence was not surrender but strategy. In the space between my thoughts and my actions, I built a sanctuary.

I began to speak with God, though I did not yet know His name.

I spoke to Him from the floor of the cellar where I hid when the beatings came. I whispered to Him from behind kitchen doors. If He answered, it was in the form of endurance, of silence that wrapped around me like a cloak.

One day, the officer's cousin visited, a merchant of perfumes whose hands smelled incongruously of sandalwood and citrus. He watched me serve the evening meal, his eyes following my movements with cold assessment.

"The black girl," he said later when they thought I could not hear. "How much?"

I was sold for fewer coins than a brass bowl.

He took me across the desert to Khartoum. The journey was burning days and knife-cold nights. I rode in the back of a cart, wedged between crates of merchandise more valuable than I. The merchant did not beat me, but his indifference cut just as deep. I was inventory, nothing more.

In Khartoum, the city where the Blue and White Nile met, I was treated better. Not well, but better. I was not beaten often. I was fed. I was even allowed to help with the younger children, whose small hands reached for me without fear.

The merchant's wife studied me with wary curiosity. "You understand more than you let on," she said once. "I see it in your eyes."

She taught me rudimentary words that tasted like stone fruit on my tongue, sweet with bitter centers. She called me little sister. It stirred something in me, a memory of my sister's hand in mine before the trees split apart and the world bled red.

There were moments in that house when I almost felt human again. When the merchant's youngest daughter climbed into my lap and touched my face with wonder. When the cook slipped me extra bread, still warm from the oven. When I caught my reflection in a copper pot and recognized, for a fleeting instant, the girl I had been.

But kindness was a thing with sharp edges. It could be withdrawn. It could bind more tightly than chains. It could make you forget what you were, a possession, a tool, a thing to be traded when its usefulness waned.

By the end of 1884, revolution encircled the city. The Mahdi's forces tightened their siege like a noose. I heard panic in the streets, saw hunger in children's eyes, smelled the rot of desperation beneath the scorching sun.

One evening, as I cleared dinner plates, I heard the master speaking with another man in urgent tones. They pored over maps by lamplight, tracing routes with fingertips that left smudges like prophecies.

"How long has she been with you?" the visitor asked, gesturing toward me.

"Nearly two years," the master replied. "But she was taken as a child. Seven, perhaps eight years ago?"

Seven years.

The number rang in my ears like a bell tolling underwater. I had not spoken that number aloud in a long time. Seven years since the raid. Seven years since my name had been stolen. Seven years of silence and servitude, of hands that struck and hands that claimed.

"And what becomes of her?" the visitor continued.

"She comes with me," said the master. "She has adapted well."

His name was Callisto Legnani. The Italian Vice Consul. And with those words, my life bent in a new direction.

He called me to his study that night. Maps covered his desk, intricate drawings of coastlines and mountains I could not identify.

"Soon," he said in our mixed tongue of Italian and Arabic, "we journey to my country. To Italia."

"Italia," I repeated. The word felt hollow and sharp like an empty gourd.

He nodded. "A different place. Cold in winter." He hesitated. "There are different laws there. Different ways."

I could not imagine what he meant. How could the world be more different than it already was? How could there be a place where the laws of masters and slaves did not apply?

But something in his voice, a note of certainty, planted a strange seed in my mind. A wondering. A question too fragile to form into words.

In the weeks that followed, I learned what it meant to serve in a household where violence was not the first language. Legnani spoke to me, not at me. He asked if I understood, rather than assuming I would obey without comprehension. He taught me words: *pane* for bread, *acqua* for water, *grazie* for thank you, *per favore* for please.

One afternoon, carrying water from the courtyard well, I stumbled. The pitcher slipped from my hands and shattered across the tiles, shards scattering like stars, water pooling in the grooves between stones.

I fell to my knees instantly, arms raised to shield my face from the beating I knew would come. My body remembered what followed broken things. My shoulders tensed, waiting for the familiar whistle of leather through air.

But Legnani only frowned.

"No," he said, shaking his head. "Get up. It is only a pitcher."

I did not move. I could not believe. Every broken object in my memory had been paid for in blood.

He knelt then, a master, kneeling, and began gathering the shards himself, placing them carefully in his palm.

"No harm," he said in halting Arabic. "No punishment. These things break. It is their nature."

I raised my eyes, searching his face for the lie, for the anger that would come later when witnesses were gone. I found none. Only a slight sadness, as if my fear itself pained him.

Slowly, I lowered my arms. Slowly, I began to breathe again.

That night, I lay on my mat and felt something shift inside me. Not the door opening. Not yet. But perhaps the first hairline crack in its surface, the first suggestion that what had been sealed might, one day, be unsealed.

Two weeks later, he summoned me again to his study.

"We leave immediately," he said. "I return to Italy. Do you wish to remain here?"

The question itself was a marvel, that my wishes should be consulted, that my preference might matter. I looked at the walls that had held me, at the window beyond which lay a city under siege, at the hands that had, against all expectation, never harmed me.

"I go with you," I said.

Something like approval flickered across his face. "It will be dangerous."

I almost smiled. As if I had not survived worse than whatever journey lay ahead.

We fled under cover of darkness—Legnani, his associate Augusto Michieli, and I. For six hundred and fifty kilometers, we traversed landscapes that shifted from dusty streets to vast emptiness where stars hung so low I felt I could pluck them from the sky. The heat of day scorched us. The cold of night sank teeth into our bones. We drank water that tasted of minerals and desperation.

Every distant figure might be Mahdist. Every shadow might conceal those who would return us to the besieged city, or worse.

Suakin rose from the horizon like a mirage—whitewashed buildings clinging to the edge of the Red Sea. The port bustled with activity: merchants and mercenaries, diplomats and deserters, all seeking passage away from the spreading revolution.

The night before we would board ship, I dreamed of water. Not the gentle streams of my childhood, where my sisters and I had splashed beneath palm fronds, but vast, hungry water that breathed like a beast. I awoke with the taste of salt on my lips, though I had not wept.

Dawn came. The inn stirred to life—trunks being hauled, servants calling, the clatter of dishes. I dressed in European clothes that still felt like a costume on my skin.

"Come," said Legnani's housekeeper. "The carriage waits."

The port swarmed with bodies and voices. Merchants haggling over shipments. Sailors shouting from deck to dock. Women weeping behind veils. And there, like a mountain rising from the harbor, waited the ship.

Its black hull gleamed in morning light, smoke pouring from its stacks in thick gray plumes. *Vittoria*, read the name painted in gilt letters across its bow. Victory. I wondered whose.

"Stay close," Legnani instructed. His face was taut with the strain of departure.

I nodded, clutching the small bundle I had been permitted to bring—a change of clothes, a hairbrush, a silver thimble the cook had given me. Meager possessions, yet more than I had owned in years.

We boarded amid a crush of passengers. The division was immediate and absolute. Legnani and Michieli disappeared into first-class cabins with polished brass fixtures. I was directed belowdecks to a cramped space shared with three other female servants.

"You're the consul's girl?" asked one, a Moroccan woman with henna-stained hands. When I nodded, she scoffed. "Lucky, then. Better than being owned by the captain. He beats his boy for sport."

The ship groaned as it pulled from the dock. I climbed to the deck to watch the shore recede. The continent of my birth shrank behind us, the sun striking the water and turning it to hammered gold. Africa shimmered, then dissolved into mist.

I felt no sorrow, no joy. Only hollowness, as if watching someone else's departure.

I looked back once. The houses stood golden against the darkening sky. No one waved. No one called my name. The water stretched before us like a dark mirror.

I turned away.

The years had been silent.

But the silence had taught me to listen.

And I was hearing something stir in the dark: a whisper, a promise, a prayer I had not known I was making. It moved within me like a second heartbeat, persistent and true.

Survive, it said. *Survive and see what comes next.*

The sea opened before us, vast and merciless. I had never seen so much water, stretching in every direction until it met the sky. This was the barrier between worlds. Not a wall or mountain range, but a liquid desert vaster than any I had crossed.

I gripped the railing. Below me, the waves churned, dark as spilled ink. Death seemed to lurk beneath each swell, patient and ancient. Yet there was something else in those waters. Something that whispered of possibility. Of distance placed between the girl I had been and the woman I might become.

The first day passed in a blur of seasickness. My stomach rebelled against the constant motion, and I spent hours bent over a bucket. The Moroccan woman brought me water and placed a cool cloth on my forehead.

"The sea takes its toll," she murmured. "You will find your sea legs soon."

By the third day, I could stand without dizziness. I was summoned to Legnani's cabin to attend his daughter, a solemn child of seven with eyes like black olives. She wanted me to comb her hair and tell her stories.

I had no stories left, only fragments of memory that rose like debris after a storm. Still, I tried, speaking in my broken Italian of birds and rivers and the shape of clouds. She listened, head tilted, then placed her small hand on my cheek.

"You're pretty," she said, "for someone so dark."

I did not know how to answer, so I said nothing. Her innocence was its own kind of cruelty.

The days blended together, marked only by bells signaling meals and watches. I learned the rhythm of the ship—the creak of timbers at dawn, the pounding of feet across deck at noon, the low murmur of prayers at dusk.

At night, I would slip away from my berth and find a quiet corner of the deck. There, under stars that seemed both strange and familiar, I would listen to the sea's constant conversation with the hull. Sometimes I thought I heard voices in it—my mother calling my true name, my sisters laughing, the village elder telling tales by firelight.

But they were ghosts. And I was becoming a ghost among ghosts.

One night, as I stood at the railing, the ship's chaplain appeared beside me. A gaunt man with skin like parchment, wearing black robes and carrying a leather-bound book.

"You watch the sea as if it holds answers," he said.

I nodded.

He opened his book. "The Bible speaks of waters that separate and waters that cleanse." He pointed to the horizon, where the first pale fingers of dawn stretched across the sky. "Perhaps that is why you watch it so intently."

He pressed something into my palm before departing. A small wooden cross. I held it long after he had gone, feeling its weight, its sharp edges. I did not know what it meant yet, but I kept it. Another small possession. Another fragment of the person I was becoming.

The rest of our journey passed without incident. The sea calmed, becoming a mirror reflecting the sun's passage. Dolphins appeared occasionally, arcing alongside the ship. Seabirds followed in our wake.

And then, one morning, land appeared.

A smudge of darkness against the pale horizon, gradually resolving into mountains, then buildings, then the intricate latticework of a harbor.

Italy.

I stood at the railing as the ship drew closer. The air smelled different here. Salt and stone and something green I could not name. Buildings rose in colors I had never seen. Ochre and terracotta and pale gold. Church bells rang across the water, their sound both foreign and strangely welcoming.

"Beautiful, yes?" said the Moroccan woman, standing beside me.

I did not answer. I was thinking of the door that had closed inside me in the storeroom in El-Obeid. Of the cold, watchful thing that had awakened there. Of the voice that whispered *survive*.

Perhaps here, in this strange land across the water, that door might open again. Perhaps the girl who had been buried beneath years of silence and suffering might find a way to breathe.

Or perhaps not. Perhaps I would remain what I had become—*spirito muto*, the mute spirit, moving through the world without leaving a trace.

Only time would tell.

The ship slipped into harbor. Sailors shouted. Ropes were thrown. The gangplank lowered with a heavy thud.

I picked up my small bundle and followed Legnani and Michieli down onto solid ground.

The earth beneath my feet did not move. For the first time in two weeks, the world held still.

I took a breath. Another.

Then I stepped forward into whatever came next.

Chapter Five

The ship entered the harbor at Genoa in the early morning of April 1885.

I had never imagined a city could look like this. Buildings rose in shades of ochre and pale gold, stacked against hillsides as if competing for space with the sky. Their facades were carved with figures—saints or angels, I could not tell—stone faces that watched our approach with eternal indifference. The harbor bristled with masts like a forest stripped of leaves, ships crowding against docks where men swarmed like ants over cargo and rope.

The air smelled of salt and fish and something else, bread, perhaps, or flowers I had no name for. Everything was louder here, sharper. Voices called in Italian, fast and musical, nothing like the measured Arabic I had learned. Church bells rang from somewhere beyond the waterfront, their sound both foreign and strangely beautiful. Even the light was different. Softer than the brutal Sudan sun, filtering through a haze that turned the morning silver.

I stood on the deck, my small bundle clutched to my chest and felt the world tilt beneath my feet. Not from the waves, but from the overwhelming strangeness of everything I saw. These people with their pale skin and elaborate dress. These buildings of stone instead of mud brick. This language flowed like water while Arabic had moved in more deliberate rhythms.

I was in Europe. The word itself felt impossible.

The gangplank lowered with a heavy thud. Passengers pressed forward, eager to reach solid ground. Legnani gestured for me to follow him, and I stepped onto Italian soil for the first time.

The cobblestones beneath my feet were smooth and cool, worn by centuries of footsteps. I stopped, unable to move forward. My legs had adjusted to the ship's motion, but that was not why I stood frozen.

This was Europe. I had crossed an ocean. I had survived the unsurvivable.

For a moment, I simply stood there, one hand pressed against a wooden post, feeling the ancient stone beneath my worn slippers, worn by centuries of feet that had never known chains, that had walked freely between market and home, between birth and death, without ever being bought or sold.

"Move along," a sailor barked in Italian, pushing past with a crate on his shoulder.

I moved. But something had shifted. However briefly, I had stood on ground where slavery was not the law. Where my body, in theory at least, belonged to me.

The thought was too large to hold. I let it slip away, following Legnani through the crowd.

Around me, the port churned with activity. Merchants haggled over crates of goods. Sailors shouted instructions. Women in dark dresses moved purposefully through the crowd, their skirts rustling. I had never seen so many white faces, so many people moving with such certainty through spaces I could not yet comprehend.

A woman waited near a stack of trunks, her dress the color of slate, her posture rigid as the carved figures on the buildings. She was younger than I had expected, perhaps thirty, with sharp features and eyes that missed nothing. Her hair was pinned severely beneath a hat that cast shadows across her face.

Maria Turina Michieli.

I did not know her name yet, but I recognized the expression she wore as she watched Legnani approach. It was the look of someone accustomed to acquiring things, assessing their quality, determining their usefulness.

Her eyes found me, traveled from my face to my worn dress to the bundle in my arms, then back again. I kept my gaze lowered, my shoulders slightly bent. Years of slavery had taught me the posture of invisibility.

"Consul Legnani," she said, her voice carrying across the space between us. "You are prompt."

"Signora Michieli." He removed his hat. "The crossing was favorable."

She stepped closer, circling me slowly. I remained still, barely breathing, as her gloved hand lifted my chin. Her touch was neither gentle nor rough, but simply matter-of-fact, as one might examine a horse before purchase. Her fingers tilted my face to one side, then the other, checking for blemishes or disease.

Then she opened my mouth, her gloved thumb pulling my lower lip down to expose my teeth.

I tasted leather and humiliation. My body went rigid, but I did not resist. This, too, was familiar. In the slave markets of Sudan, buyers had examined me the same way—as livestock, as merchandise, as anything but human.

"Good," Maria said, releasing me. "Healthy."

"How old?" she asked Legnani.

"Perhaps sixteen. It is difficult to say with certainty."

"And her disposition?"

"Quiet. Obedient. She has served my household without difficulty these past two years."

Maria's fingers released my face. She stepped back, arms crossed beneath her breast. "My son grows worse. The fever returned three nights ago. He cries until dawn, and the nursemaid has fallen ill herself. I cannot manage both children and the household without help."

"I understand your need is urgent."

"More than urgent. Desperate." Her voice dropped, taking on a note of something almost raw. "Menotti is so small, so fragile. And Mimmina asks constantly when we will settle, when her life will become normal again. They both need constancy."

Legnani nodded slowly. "Bakhita has cared for children before. She is gentle with them."

"You vouch for her, then?"

"I do." He paused, his hand moving to adjust his collar. "But I ask that you remember she has endured much in her short life. I have not raised my hand to her, not once. She responds better to kindness than to force."

Maria's eyebrows rose slightly. "I am not a barbarian, Consul. I require assistance, not a whipping post."

"Of course. Forgive me. I only meant—" He stopped, seeming to search for words. "She has proven loyal. I would not wish to see that loyalty broken through unnecessary harshness."

Something passed between them then, a tension I could not fully interpret. Maria's expression hardened, then softened again, settling into professional courtesy.

"Your concern is noted," she said. "She will be well-treated in my household, provided she performs her duties satisfactorily."

Legnani's shoulders lowered slightly, as if releasing a weight. "Then we are agreed. She will accompany you to Zianigo."

"Today," Maria confirmed. "The carriage is arranged."

That was when I understood. I was being given away.

Not sold. No money changed hands, no papers were signed. But transferred, nonetheless. From one household to another, from one form of service to another. The realization moved through me slowly, like cold water seeping through cloth.

Legnani, who had asked if I wished to come to Italy. Legnani, who had knelt to gather the broken pitcher shards. Legnani, who had never struck me.

He was giving me away.

I felt the door inside me, the one that had begun to show the first hairline crack, seal itself once more. Not with the violent closing that had happened in El-Obeid, but with something quieter. A settling. An acceptance of what I had always known but briefly forgotten: kindness from masters was conditional. Ownership, however gentle, was still ownership.

I was a thing to be transferred when convenience required it.

Legnani turned to me then, his expression difficult to read. "Bakhita," he said in Arabic. "You will go with Signora Michieli. She has children who need care. You will serve them well, yes?"

"Yes," I replied, the word automatic.

He reached into his coat and withdrew something, a small wooden crucifix on a simple cord. The same cross the ship's chaplain had given me, or perhaps another like it. He pressed it into my palm.

"Keep this," he said quietly. "It may bring you comfort."

I closed my fingers around it, feeling its edges bite into my skin.

"Thank you," I whispered.

He nodded once, then turned back to Maria, speaking again in rapid Italian I could not follow. They discussed logistics—departure time, directions to Zianigo, when he might visit. Their voices faded to background noise as I stood holding the crucifix, its weight slight but somehow significant.

Within the hour, I was seated in a carriage beside Maria Michieli, my bundle at my feet, watching Genoa recede behind us as we traveled inland.

The journey to Zianigo took most of the day.

We traveled through countryside so green it almost hurt to look at. Fields stretched endlessly, dotted with farms and stone houses whose red-tiled roofs gleamed in the spring sun. Flowers bloomed along the roadside in colors I had never seen in such abundance—purple and yellow and white, nodding in the breeze as our carriage passed.

In Darfur, green had meant the rainy season. It had meant survival, celebration, the promise of another year. Here, green was simply April.

Water was so abundant they wasted it on decoration, on gardens that served no purpose but beauty. I touched the shawl Maria had wordlessly handed me when we departed and felt the ghost of desert thirst in my throat.

The air smelled of earth and growth, of water and something sweet I could not identify. It was cooler here than in Genoa, and infinitely cooler than Sudan. I found myself shivering despite the shawl.

Maria sat across from me, her face turned toward the window, seemingly absorbed in the passing landscape. She had not spoken since we left the port except to give brief instructions to the driver. Occasionally, she would sigh—small, tired exhalations that suggested a weariness deeper than physical exhaustion.

I studied her when I thought she would not notice. Her dress, though somber in color, was finely made, with small buttons down the bodice and lace at the collar. Her hands, clasped in her lap, were pale and smooth, unmarked by labor. She wore a simple gold band on one finger. A wife, then. A mother. A woman of some means, traveling with a servant to care for her ailing son and lonely daughter.

We passed stone farmhouses with smoke rising from chimneys. Families lived there, I supposed. Families who had always lived there, whose children would live there after them, whose names stretched back generations on the same plot of land. I tried to imagine such permanence and could not. I had no land. No true name. No certainty of where I would be tomorrow, let alone in seven years.

The carriage hit a rough section of road, jostling us both. Maria's hand shot out to steady herself against the side panel. For a moment, our eyes met. She did not look away immediately, and neither did I. Something passed between us—not warmth, exactly, but perhaps acknowledgment. Two women in a carriage, each carrying burdens the other could not fully see.

Then she turned back to the window, and the moment passed.

By late afternoon, we reached Zianigo.

The town was small, little more than a cluster of buildings surrounding a church with a bell tower that rose like a pointing finger toward heaven. The streets were narrow, cobbled, and lined with houses whose shuttered windows gave them a closed, secretive appearance.

The church bells rang as we entered the town. Six deep tones that resonated across the countryside. For a moment, I was seven years old again, running through Olgossa while the village drums called us to gather. Different sounds, different gods, but the same human impulse: to mark time, to call the community, to make meaning from the passage of hours.

A few people paused to watch our carriage pass with the mild curiosity of those for whom strangers are uncommon but not threatening. I wondered what they saw. A wealthy woman returning to her villa. A dark-skinned servant, exotic and foreign. Property that could speak and walk but was not quite human in their eyes.

We continued beyond the town center to an estate on its outskirts. The villa stood behind iron gates, a substantial structure of pale stone with a red-tiled roof and arched windows. Gardens surrounded it. Not the wild, water-starved plants of Sudan, but cultivated beds of flowers and herbs, neatly trimmed hedges, gravel paths that wound between them like veins.

The carriage stopped before the entrance. Maria stepped down first, and I followed, my legs stiff from hours of sitting. A servant appeared, an older woman with gray hair beneath a white cap, and took Maria's traveling case without a word.

"Bakhita will sleep in the nursery," Maria instructed in Italian. The older woman glanced at me, her expression neutral, then nodded.

I followed them inside.

The villa's interior was dim after the brightness outside, my eyes adjusting slowly to reveal a space both grand and intimate. Tiled floors, plastered walls, a staircase that curved upward to the second floor. Religious paintings hung in gilded frames. The Madonna and child, Christ on the cross, saints I could not name performing miracles or suffering martyrdoms. Furniture of dark wood gleamed with polish. The air smelled of beeswax and lavender and something faintly medicinal.

Everything was clean, ordered, prosperous. And utterly foreign.

"This way," Maria said, already climbing the stairs. I hurried to follow, my worn slippers making soft sounds against the tiles.

She led me to a room on the second floor. The door was ajar, and from within came a thin, persistent wailing. The cry of a very young child in distress.

Maria's face tightened. She pushed open the door.

The nursery was smaller than I expected, but well-appointed. A cradle stood near the window, a small bed against one wall, a chair beside a cold fireplace. Toys lay scattered on the floor—a wooden horse, a rag doll, colored blocks. And in the cradle, thrashing against his blankets, was Menotti.

He was tiny, perhaps six months old, his face red and twisted with crying. Sweat dampened his sparse dark hair. His little fists waved aimlessly, and even from the doorway, I could see the fever flush on his cheeks.

Maria moved to him immediately, lifting him with practiced care. She murmured in Italian, words I did not understand but whose tone was universal, the soothing sounds a mother makes to a suffering child. He continued to wail, his body rigid in her arms.

"He has been like this for days," she said, not looking at me. "Nothing helps. Not milk, not cool cloths, not rocking. Nothing."

I set down my bundle and approached slowly. "May I?" I asked in broken Italian, gesturing toward the child.

Maria hesitated, then carefully transferred him to my arms.

He was so light, so fragile. I could feel the heat radiating from his small body, the rapid flutter of his heartbeat against my chest. His cries did not diminish, but something in his thrashing eased slightly, as if the change itself provided momentary distraction.

I began to rock gently, finding the rhythm that mothers in Olgossa had used with fretful infants. Side to side, a small movement, steady as breathing. I hummed, not words, just sound, a melody half-remembered from childhood.

Gradually, his cries softened. Not stopping but losing their sharp edge of panic. His eyes, glassy with fever, found my face and held there, as if trying to understand this new presence.

"You have a gift," Maria said quietly. Her voice held something I had not heard before, relief, perhaps, or hope.

I did not respond. I simply continued rocking, humming, holding this fragile life that had been placed in my care.

After what might have been minutes or an hour, Menotti's eyes finally closed. His breathing evened into the deeper rhythm of sleep, though his body still radiated heat. I lowered myself carefully into the chair, unwilling to risk waking him.

Maria watched from beside the window, her arms crossed, her expression unreadable. Then she moved closer, looking down at her sleeping son with something raw on her face.

"I thought I would be better at this," she said quietly, more to herself than to me. "A mother should know how to comfort her own child. But he only cries harder when I hold him. As if he knows I don't know how." She stopped, her jaw tightening. "You will sleep here. In the nursery. Menotti wakes often in the night. You must attend to him whenever he cries."

"Yes, signora."

"My daughter, Mimmina, sleeps in the adjacent room. She is four. Curious. Active. You will care for her as well during the day while I manage the household."

"Yes, signora."

"There are other servants, but few. We are establishing ourselves here, and funds are..." She paused, seeming to catch herself. "We are managing carefully. You will have duties beyond the children, helping in the kitchen, mending, whatever is needed. Do you understand?"

"Yes, signora."

She studied me for a long moment, as if trying to penetrate the mask of compliance I wore. Whatever she sought, she did not find it. Or perhaps she did, and it satisfied her.

"Good," she said at last. "I will have supper sent up. You may eat after Menotti is settled for the night."

She left, closing the door softly behind her.

I sat in the chair, holding the sleeping child, and looked around the room that would be my world for however long this new captivity lasted. The older servant returned with a tray, bread, cheese, some kind of thin soup, and set it on a small table. She gestured to a pallet that had been placed on the floor near the cradle.

"You sleep there," she said in heavily accented Italian, speaking slowly as if to a child. "You don't leave the nursery at night. The children might need you."

She pointed to a chamber pot in the corner, then left without waiting for acknowledgment.

It was not a room. It was a cage with better furnishings.

The fading light through the window cast long shadows across the floor. Outside, I heard birds singing, their songs different from the birds of home, but birds nonetheless.

I thought of Legnani, perhaps already back in Genoa, relieved to have discharged his responsibility. I thought of the crucifix in my bundle, its meaning still opaque to me. I thought of the door inside me, firmly closed now, protecting what little remained of my core self from further disappointment.

New shores. New chains.

The landscape had changed, the language had changed, the color of my master's skin had changed. But I remained what I had always been., Property, passed from hand to hand, my purpose defined by others' needs.

Menotti stirred in my arms, making small, distressed sounds even in sleep. I adjusted my hold, resuming the gentle rocking, the wordless humming.

Outside, the church bell in Zianigo rang again. A single toll marking the half hour. In Sudan, evening prayers would be sounding. In my village, if it still existed, fires would be lit, families gathering to share the day's end.

But I was here, in this strange land, holding a fevered child who knew nothing of deserts or chains or lost names. Who knew only his small suffering and his need for comfort.

I could give him that, at least. Whatever else had been taken from me, I still possessed the ability to soothe a crying child.

It was something. Perhaps it was enough.

The evening passed in a rhythm of waking and sleeping. I fed Menotti when the older servant brought milk. I changed him when needed. I rocked him through two more crying spells, humming the melodies of Olgossa until he quieted. Between these tasks, I ate the food that had been left for me and unpacked my small bundle—a change of clothes, the silver thimble from the cook, the wooden crucifix.

I was slipping the crucifix's cord over my neck when I heard a small sound from the doorway.

A face appeared in the shadows, wide brown eyes beneath a tangle of dark curls, a white nightgown trailing on the floor.

"Are you the African?" the child whispered.

I froze, uncertain whether I should acknowledge her. But she stepped into the room before I could decide, bare feet padding across the tiles.

She was small, perhaps four years old, with her mother's sharp features softened by youth. She tilted her head, studying me with unguarded curiosity.

"Mama says you came on a ship," she said. "From across the sea. Is that true?"

"Yes," I replied carefully.

"Were there storms? Did you see whales?"

"There was much water. No whales."

She looked disappointed, then brightened. "Will you tell me stories about lions? And elephants? Mama says you have elephants in Africa."

"I do not know stories of lions," I said. In truth, I had seen lions only in the distance, and elephants not at all. The Sudan of my captivity had been cities and compounds, not wilderness.

"Oh." Her small face fell. Then she moved closer, looking up at me with something like determination. "What's your real name?"

The question pierced something inside me. My real name. The one stolen seven years ago, the one I could barely remember the shape of anymore. The one my mother had spoken, that had died with her or been buried so deep I could no longer reach it.

"Bakhita," I said. It was all I had left.

"Bakhita," she repeated, mangling the pronunciation slightly. "I'm Mimmina. That's not my real name either. It's Alice. But everyone calls me Mimmina." She reached out and touched my arm, her small fingers tracing one of the raised scars visible beneath my sleeve. "What are these?"

I pulled back instinctively. "Decoration. From before."

"They're beautiful," she said with the simple honesty of childhood. "Like flowers."

They were not like flowers. They were marks of ownership, of cruelty, of a woman's vanity carved into my flesh. But I did not correct her.

"You should be asleep," I said instead.

"I heard Menotti crying. I wanted to see if he was better." She peered at the cradle where her brother slept. "Is he?"

"The fever has not broken yet. But he sleeps now."

"Good." She yawned, suddenly looking very young and very tired. "Will you be here tomorrow?"

"Yes."

"Then we'll be friends," she declared, as if friendship were simply a matter of proximity and decision. She turned to leave, then paused at the doorway. "I'm glad you're here, Bakhita. This house has been sad. Maybe you'll make it happier."

She disappeared before I could respond, her small feet pattering down the hallway.

I stood in the empty nursery, holding the crucifix, feeling something shift inside me that I could not name. Not hope. I could not afford hope. But something.

A child who asked my name instead of ignoring it. Who called scars beautiful instead of shameful. Who declared friendship as easily as breathing.

Perhaps not everything in this new captivity would be like the old.

That night, after Menotti had been fed and settled and had woken twice more before falling into deeper sleep, I lay on the thin pallet near the cradle. The villa was quiet around me, only the occasional creak of settling wood and the distant sound of Maria moving in another part of the house.

I took the crucifix from around my neck and held it in the darkness, tracing its shape with my fingertips. The ship's chaplain had said something about waters that separate and waters that cleanse. Legnani had given me this as though it held some power or promise I could not yet grasp.

What was this symbol? I knew it was sacred to these Europeans, that it hung in every room of this house, that the building with the bell tower in town was dedicated to whatever it represented. But its meaning remained closed to me, like a book in a language I had not learned.

I thought of the conversation with God I had begun in the Turkish officer's cellar. The nameless presence I had whispered to when all other hope failed. Was this crucifix connected to that? Was the God I had spoken to in desperation the same one these Italians served?

I did not know. I had no way of knowing.

But I kept the crucifix anyway, slipping the cord back over my head. In Sudan, I had worn scars I did not choose. Here, I wore a symbol I did not understand. Both marked me as belonging to something I had not chosen.

But the crucifix was lighter than the scars. And I had put it on myself.

That difference, however small, felt like something.

Menotti whimpered in his sleep. I rose quietly, went to the cradle, placed a hand on his small back. His skin was cooler than before, not normal yet, but better. His breathing was steady, deep. He quieted under my touch, settling back into sleep.

The fever was breaking.

I stood over him in the darkness, this fragile Italian child who knew nothing of deserts or chains. Who cried when he needed comfort and received it. Who would grow up free, never knowing what it meant to be property, to have no say in where you lived or who owned you or what was done to your body.

What would that be like, I wondered. To grow up expecting the world to care when you cried.

I would never know. But perhaps, by caring for him, I could help him keep that expectation a little longer. Perhaps that was enough of a purpose to fill the hollow places inside me.

Before returning to my pallet, I moved quietly to the nursery door and tried the handle. It opened easily. No lock, no bolt. I could walk out if I wished. Down the stairs, through the entrance, into the Italian night.

But where would I go? I spoke barely any Italian. I had no money. I wore the invisible collar that marked all servants—foreign, dark-skinned, female, obviously belonging to someone else. Even in a country without legal slavery, I would be returned to my master. Or worse.

The door was unlocked. But I was not free.

I closed it softly and returned to my pallet.

Tomorrow, I would meet Mimmina properly in daylight. Tomorrow, I would begin to learn the rhythms of this new household, the expectations of this new mistress, the boundaries of this new form of captivity.

Tomorrow, I would continue surviving.

But tonight, in the darkness of an Italian nursery, wearing a symbol I did not understand around my neck, having soothed a child whose fever had finally broken, I allowed myself one small moment of wondering. Not hope. I could not afford hope. But wondering.

What if the chaplain had been right? What if crossing the sea had been more than just changing location? What if something was waiting here that I could not yet see, something that might, against all probability, lead toward a door opening rather than closing?

I did not believe it. But I wondered.

And sometimes, when survival is all you have, wondering is enough to carry you through to morning.

I closed my eyes.

Through the nursery window, I could see a single star, brighter than the others, or perhaps just more visible through the foreign sky. In Olgossa, my mother had told me that stars were the eyes of ancestors, watching over us.

I did not know if my ancestors could see me here, in this strange land where I wore a cross I didn't understand and cared for children who were not mine.

But the star was there. I was here. And Menotti's breathing was steady and strong.

For now, that would have to be enough.

Outside, the night deepened over Zianigo, and somewhere in the distance, a dog barked three times before falling silent.

Chapter Six

The ship carried me away from everything I had known in Africa, toward everything I would become in Italy. We departed under an unexceptional sun, but I was no longer the girl who had arrived in that other harbor, years before, in chains.

Maria kept to the upper quarters, her son feverish in her lap. I remained below deck with the servants, summoned when she tired of his moans. Menotti clutched at me with desperate fingers. He would not eat unless I was near.

We sailed through days of salt-stung wind until the air turned cold and the light grew weak. Then Venice appeared, a smear of gold and gray rising from the lagoon, dreamlike yet already weighted with dread.

The city rose from the sea like a cathedral built on bones.

The lagoon glittered under pale winter sun. The air smelled of brine and old incense, of wet stone and something darker, the particular rot of a place where water and earth have made their uneasy peace. Buildings loomed in shades of ochre and gold, their facades peeling like old masks. I had never seen so many windows, eyes without souls, watching silently.

Bells rang in the distance, slow and mournful. Pigeons scattered like ashes across an unseen square.

We disembarked into chaos. Porters shouted for fares, customs officials demanded papers, families reunited in tearful embraces. Augusto Michieli shepherded his household through the crowd with practiced efficiency. I followed Maria, my bundle clutched to my chest, my eyes wide with a wonder I did not trust.

Venice was a place of water and stone, of bridges that arched like the backs of cats, of narrow alleys that twisted like secrets. The canals reflected buildings in fractured, dancing images. Gondolas glided past, black as beetles, carrying passengers wrapped in furs against the winter chill. Everything shimmered, light on water, water on stone, until I could not tell what was solid and what was only reflection.

The air itself felt different. Heavier. Older. Laden with stories I could not read.

We were taken to a house in the village of Zianigo, near the town of Mirano. There the Michieli palazzo stood, silent and severe, its façade stained with age and salt. No welcome awaited me, only the creak of ancient doors and the averted eyes of servants who would not acknowledge my presence.

In this way, I settled into my new home.

Maria kept me close, but not as a companion. I was a shadow in her household, summoned at will, dismissed without notice. Neither slave nor servant, but in purpose I was both. They fed me, clothed me, kept me from the streets, always with the air of *noblesse oblige*, as if I were some charitable burden they had graciously assumed.

Their daughter, little Mimmina, took an immediate liking to me. She was perhaps four years old, with dark curls that refused taming and a gap between her front teeth that showed when she smiled. She tugged at my skirts and asked questions in rapid Italian I could barely follow. She liked my hair, though the mistress insisted it be pulled back and bound tightly so I would not draw attention.

Sometimes Mimmina would press her small palm against my scarred forearm and trace the patterns there with one finger, whispering, "*Bella*"—beautiful—as if she truly believed it. In those moments, something shifted in my chest, some small loosening of the bands that had held my heart captive for so long.

At night I slept on a mat near Menotti's room, beside the hearth. When he coughed, I sat upright. When he cried, I sang to him in broken Italian, fragments of lullabies I had learned on the ship, words I did not fully understand but that seemed to soothe him. He called me Bakhita, though they had tried to give me other names.

Moretta. Little dark one.

La Schiava. The slave.

I did not answer to either.

Signora Michieli never struck me. She never needed to. Her eyes were punishment enough.

And in that house of foreign saints and cold marble floors, I came to understand I had been passed from one cage to another.

Signor Augusto Michieli was not a consul, as I had first thought, but a merchant of silk and fine goods, and his family had the quiet pride of people who had never gone without. They dressed in dark wool and wore their sorrow like jewelry. Their eldest son had died of fever two winters past. His portrait hung in the entryway, pale and unsmiling, with a gaze that followed you down the corridor. Sometimes I wondered if he watched me because he, too, had known what it meant to be trapped, by illness rather than chains, but trapped nonetheless.

I learned silence once more, but a different kind.

In Africa, silence had meant survival; the erasure of self to avoid notice, to avoid pain. In Zianigo, silence meant obedience. I listened to the clatter of porcelain at breakfast, to the measured tapping of heels across tiled floors, to the whisper of rosary beads passing through fingers at dusk. I learned the rhythms of this household as I had learned the rhythms of others—by watching, by listening, by making myself small enough to slip through the cracks of their attention.

The servants spoke little to me, but I overheard their conversations in the kitchen, in the laundry room, in the corridor outside my mistress's chamber. I learned that silence here had its own language. What was spoken and what was carefully left unsaid.

But at night, I remembered the branding.

I felt again the iron press of fire on skin, the knife's precise agony tracing patterns I had not chosen. I would wake with the sheets clutched in my fists, the candle flickering shadows across the frescoed ceiling, my breath shallow and quick until the present reasserted itself.

I was in Italy now. The cutting was years behind me.

Yet my body remembered what my mind tried to forget.

Father Antonio came often.

He was from Verona, a Canossian priest with soft eyes and hands always folded, as if perpetually in prayer. He spoke to me gently, in slow Italian, and when I did not answer he spoke still, not forcing response, but offering words like bread to someone starving.

"Do not be afraid to learn," he said once, after Mass in the small chapel adjacent to the house. "Your soul has not forgotten how to speak."

I did not understand all his words then. But something in them struck like a chord long silent—a vibration I felt more than heard, a resonance in some deep place I had thought entirely dead.

One morning, he gave me a small book. It bore the sign of the cross on its cover, the pages thin as leaves. I could not read it, but I carried it with me, hidden in the folds of my apron. I would touch it sometimes, like a charm, though I did not yet believe in its power.

The household grew used to me, but I was never one of them. When visitors came, I was hidden behind doors or made to serve in silence. My skin marked me. My silence marked me more.

One evening, as snow fell soft and soundless upon the city, I wandered into the chapel near the servants' quarters. The candles flickered like trapped stars. There, on the wall above the altar, hung a crucifix, the first I truly noticed, the first I allowed myself to see.

I did not know the man on the cross.

But his face spoke of pain. Of suffering borne in silence. Of a body marked and broken, exposed for all to see yet somehow still possessing dignity. A dignity that transcended the horror of what had been done to it.

I stood there a long while, the hush of the chapel wrapping around me like warm wool. My heart ached, but it did not collapse. It burned, a slow, patient fire, neither comforting nor entirely painful. Just... awake.

I raised one hand, almost without thinking, and pressed my palm against my chest where the oldest scars lay beneath my dress. His wounds were visible. Mine were hidden. But perhaps, perhaps, that meant something.

The crossing had changed me. The sea had not claimed me, though there were nights I had wished it would. Instead, it had carried me, wave by wave, to this strange shore where nothing was familiar except the language of suffering.

It was not yet faith that stirred within me.

But it was the beginning of something that moved beneath the ash of all I had endured. A stirring so faint I might have imagined it, yet persistent enough that I could not entirely deny its presence.

For the first time in many years, I wanted to know something beyond survival.

I wanted to know the name of the God who bled.

Chapter Seven

Winter arrived and then deepened. In the canals, the water turned thick and sluggish, dark as spilled ink. Frost etched delicate patterns across the windowpanes of the Michieli villa, like ancient script I could not decipher. When I touched it with my fingertip, it melted, leaving wet tracks like tears. I wrapped my hands in wool, but the cold crept in anyway, stealing sleep from my bones.

I worked. I served. I obeyed.

But within me, something dangerous grew.

It began with a question I could not name, not spoken, not shaped in words, but alive nonetheless, buried like a coal beneath years of ash. I felt it in the chapel's hush, in the way candlelight danced across the crucifix, casting shadows that moved like reaching hands. I felt it in Father Antonio's voice when he read from the Book, not to me, but near me, as if he knew the sound would find its mark.

He read of a shepherd searching for one lost sheep.

Of a servant forgiven an impossible debt.

Of a man nailed to a cross, praying for those who killed him.

I did not understand. But I listened.

The Michieli home stood like a sentinel, its marble façade weathered by centuries of salt and wind. Inside, velvet drapes hung heavy, absorbing light and sound. The floors were inlaid with stone patterns, spirals and stars that I traced with my eyes as I scrubbed them clean each morning. The ceilings arched high above, painted with scenes of angels and clouds that seemed to move in the flickering lamplight, wings stretching toward heaven or perhaps only toward the illusion of it.

Signor Michieli was seldom home, always traveling for his silk trade. The mistress, Maria Turina, kept to her rooms, emerging only to issue orders or receive visitors. She was not cruel to me. Not like the others had been. But her indifference cut in its own way—the casual dismissal of my presence, as if I were furniture, useful but unremarkable.

Only little Mimmina sought me out.

She was nine years old, with hair like burnished copper and eyes that held a child's innocent curiosity. She followed me as I worked, asking questions I could barely understand, much less answer.

"Why is your skin so dark?" she asked once, as I folded linens in the drawing room.

I kept my head down, my hands moving mechanically through the fabric. I had no words to explain what I had not chosen.

"I like it," she decided, touching my hand with small, pale fingers. "It's like the chocolate Papa brings from Milan."

Something twisted in my chest. Not quite pain. Not quite gratitude. Children meant well, but their words still named me as *other*—sweet, perhaps, but consumable, foreign, meant to be enjoyed by those who could afford such luxuries.

Still, she was kind. And kindness was rare enough that I did not correct her.

She taught me words—*tavolo* for table, *finestra* for window, *gatto* for the striped cat that prowled the kitchen. And each night, lying on my straw pallet, I repeated one word she had taught me: *Dio.*

God.

I did not know if He heard me. But the name made something inside me settle, as if an invisible hand had rested gently on my back.

One day, the mistress sent me with Mimmina to the Canossian Sisters' Institute of the Catechumens near San Zaccaria. The child was to begin lessons, and I was to accompany her as nursemaid.

The convent walls were high and white, flanked by bare trees whose branches scratched against the winter sky like skeletal fingers. The sisters wore black veils and moved like shadows—soft-footed, precise, their silence somehow different from the silence I had learned. Theirs felt chosen. Mine had been beaten into place.

One of them smiled at me.

It was not the smile of a mistress evaluating property, nor of a merchant's wife feigning charity. It held no pity, no curiosity.

It held recognition.

As if she saw not what had been done to me, but what remained despite it.

I lowered my eyes, unsettled by the unfamiliar weight of being seen.

Inside, the halls smelled of beeswax and old books, of bread baking somewhere deep in the building's heart. There were crucifixes in every room. I counted them as I walked, as though by doing so I might divine some meaning—or perhaps simply to focus on something other than the strange tightness in my throat.

One of the sisters, Sorella Maria, approached me with a basket of bread and gestured toward a bench. "Sit," she said in simple Italian. "The child will be some time."

I hesitated. Commands I understood. Invitations confused me.

She smiled again. patient, unhurried, and set the bread beside me. "It is not a trick," she said softly. "Only kindness."

I sat. My hands trembled as I reached for the bread.

"You are from Africa?" she asked.

I nodded.

"How long in Venice?"

"Three months." The words were still awkward on my tongue, the Italian syllables sharp where my first language had been rounded and soft.

She nodded, then touched the cross at her breast. "God sees you," she said. "Even when others do not."

The words pierced something I had thought armored beyond reach. I turned away, afraid she would see the trembling in my face, the dangerous stirring of something I could not afford to feel.

Hope was a luxury. Hope was a trap.

That day, I sat in the back of the classroom while the children traced letters across parchment. I could not read, but I watched the shapes, the curves of language like rivers winding toward something I could not name. In Sudan, writing had been magic, a secret code of the masters. In the Turkish merchant's house, it had been a tool I was forbidden to touch.

Here, among the sisters, it seemed a door left unlocked.

When Sorella Maria offered to teach me, I could not speak. My throat closed around words that would not come. I only nodded.

And so, each week, I returned.

For the first lesson, she gave me a slate and chalk, and I held them as if they might burn me.

"Your name first," Sorella Maria said, positioning the chalk in my fingers. "B-A-K-H-I-T-A."

I stared at the blank surface. My hand would not move.

She waited. No impatience. No anger. Just presence, steady as stone.

"I..." My voice cracked. "If I make mistake..."

"Then you make a mistake." Her tone was matter-of-fact. "And we try again."

I had been beaten for mistakes. Starved for mistakes. Branded for existing.

My hand shook violently now, the chalk chattering against the slate.

"Look at me," she said gently.

I forced my eyes up to meet hers.

"You are safe here. Do you understand? Whatever you write, however you write it, you are safe."

Something broke inside me then, not loudly, but like ice cracking beneath weight it can no longer bear.

I pressed the chalk to the slate and drew the first letter. Crooked. Uncertain.

B.

"Good," she said. "Again."

By the end of that first lesson, I had written my name three times. Each letter was crooked, childish, trembling. But they were mine.

When I made mistakes, she did not strike me.

When I asked to learn more, she did not laugh.

For the first time in my life, I was not a beast to be beaten or a tool to be sold.

I was a soul learning to speak.

In the church attached to the convent, I saw a painting of the Madonna. Her face was serene, her eyes downcast, but there was strength in her posture, in the way she held the child to her breast.

She was dark.

Not like me, but darker than the pale Venetians—olive-skinned, with eyes like pools of shadow. I found myself returning to her, drawn by something I could not articulate, standing before her until my legs ached and the bells rang for vespers.

"*La Madonna Nera*," Sorella Maria told me one day, appearing quietly at my side. "The Black Madonna."

She explained that this image was revered across Italy, that Mary was sometimes depicted with dark skin, that holiness wore many faces.

I stared up at the painting, at the Madonna's calm, compassionate gaze.

But not my face, I thought bitterly. *Not someone carved like cattle, marked as property.*

As if reading my thoughts, Sorella Maria said softly, "She, too, knew suffering. She watched her son tortured. Killed. She could do nothing to stop it."

I looked at her sharply.

"Pain does not make us unworthy of love," the sister continued. "Sometimes it makes us capable of greater love than those who have never suffered."

I wanted to believe her. But belief felt like reaching for something just beyond my grasp, my fingers closing on empty air.

The weeks passed. I learned more words—*pace* and *luce*, peace and light. The chalk dust coated my fingers white, and sometimes I stared at my hands, at the contrast of white against black, wondering which was the mask and which was real.

I continued my duties at the villa, carrying water, sweeping floors, preparing meals, attending Mimmina. But my mind was elsewhere, in the quiet rooms of the convent, in the pages of the book I was slowly learning to read, in the face of the man on the cross who, like me, had suffered.

One evening, as I helped the cook prepare the evening meal, I cut my finger on a knife.

The blood welled up, bright against my skin.

The cook clucked her tongue and wrapped it in cloth, but I stood transfixed, staring at the red soaking through white linen.

My blood was the same color as theirs.

The same color as the blood in the paintings of Christ, the blood that ran from his hands, his feet, his side. The blood they said had washed away sin, had purchased salvation, had proven love stronger than death.

If my blood was the same...

If his wounds and mine shared the same red...

The thought was too large, too dangerous. I pushed it away, but it stayed, hovering at the edges of my mind like a visitor waiting at the door.

When Mimmina fell ill with fever one week, the mistress sent for a priest. He came in the night, carrying a leather case and smelling of wine and wax. He sat by the child's bed and placed his hand on her forehead, murmuring prayers in Latin.

I watched from the doorway, seeing not power but tenderness in his gestures.

When he turned to leave, he saw me and paused.

"You are the African girl," he said.

I nodded, my body tensing automatically.

"Do you pray for the child?"

I did not know how to answer. Prayer had been a formless thing for me. A cry without shape, a name repeated in darkness, a desperate hope cast into a void that might or might not hear.

He seemed to understand my silence. He reached into his pocket and pressed something into my palm.

A small wooden rosary, its beads smooth from years of handling.

I flinched at the touch, then stilled, shocked by my own reaction. He had not hurt me. He had given me something.

"Ten Aves," he said, miming the counting of beads. "For the child. God hears all languages."

That night, alone in my corner, I ran my fingers over the beads, whispering the sounds I had heard others make: *Ave Maria, gratia plena.* I did not know their meaning. But I felt their rhythm, their weight, the way they marked time and intention.

As I counted, something inside me counted too. The years of silence, the moments of mercy, the long road that had brought me here.

When I finished, I pressed the rosary to my heart and whispered one word: "*Dio.*"

And for the first time, I felt as though I might be heard.

In the convent library one afternoon, while Mimmina practiced her letters, Sorella Maria showed me a book with my name written on a page.

Not *Bakhita.*

Below it, in her careful hand, she had written: *Isaiah 43:1*

"What does it say?" I asked.

She opened another book, running her finger down the page until she found the passage. Then she read aloud, slowly, so I could follow:

"*Non temere, perché io ti ho riscattato, ti ho chiamato per nome: tu sei mia.*"

"*Do not fear, for I have redeemed you. I have called you by name. You are mine.*"

My throat closed. I could not speak.

"Do you know your true name?" she asked gently. "The one from before?"

I shook my head. "They called me Bakhita," I whispered. "But before... I do not remember."

The loss of it struck me freshly then. Not just my name, but my sister who had last spoken it, my mother who had given it, the entire world in which that name had meaning.

Sorella Maria took my hands in hers, the first touch freely given, not taken, in more years than I could count.

"God remembers," she said. "Even what we forget. He knows the name your mother called you. And He calls you by it still."

That night, I dreamed of my village. I saw the circle of huts, the acacia trees, the children playing in the dust. I saw my mother grinding grain, singing softly. I saw my father returning from the hunt. I saw my sister reaching for my hand.

But when I reached back, my hand passed through hers like smoke.

I woke with tears on my face—the first I had shed in years.

Winter softened. In the canals, ice gave way to flowing water. In the gardens behind the villa, green shoots pushed through soil still hard with cold. Spring crept forward with tentative steps, as if uncertain of its welcome.

And in my heart, the seed continued to grow.

Nourished by the kindness of the sisters. By the stories I was learning to read. By the mystery that beckoned from behind the veil of ritual and symbol. By the radical possibility that I might be more than what had been done to me.

That I might be beloved.

The thought terrified me. But I could not unthink it.

One morning, as I swept the courtyard of the villa, I found myself humming. Not a song from my childhood, those were lost, but a melody I had heard the sisters sing. A hymn whose words I did not yet know, but whose music had taken root anyway.

I stopped mid-stroke, startled by the sound of my own voice.

When had I last sung?

When had I last allowed myself joy, even this small, fragile kind?

I looked up at the sky, clear, pale blue, infinite. And I felt something I had not felt since the forest, since my sister's hand slipped from mine.

I felt the faint stirring of hope.

Not certainty. Not peace. Not the absence of fear.

But hope. Stubborn. Tender. Alive.

For the first time since the forest, I allowed myself to imagine a life beyond survival.

Chapter Eight

I stood against the wall during dinner, hands folded, waiting to clear the next course. The family was discussing their spring travel plans when Signor Michieli set down his wineglass with finality. "We are returning to Africa."

The crystal rang against the wood.

My hands, folded at the small of my back, began to tremble. I pressed them harder together until the knuckles went white. Africa. The word alone.

"When?" The mistress's voice cut through the dining room like a blade on porcelain.

"Three weeks. The spring winds favor a crossing."

Little Mimmina clapped, the sound too bright, too loud. "Will there be lions, Papa? Elephants?"

He smiled. "Perhaps, my dove."

I stared at the half-cleared table. A smear of olive oil caught the candlelight. My throat closed. I couldn't swallow.

"Africa holds many wonders," he continued.

Yes. And chains. And auctions. And men who measured your worth in coins.

Later, alone in the kitchen with the stacked porcelain, my hands shook so badly I had to set the plates down before they shattered.

The mistress came the next morning. Her silk skirts whispered against stone as she entered the kitchen. Unusual for her. She never visited where the work happened.

"You heard my husband."

I nodded, kept my eyes on the floor where they belonged.

"The journey will be difficult." A pause. "The child has grown attached to you."

My heart kicked against bone.

"You will accompany us. To Africa." She said it as if offering a gift. "Prepare yourself."

The floor seemed to tilt. I gripped the edge of the worktable.

"Do you understand?"

"Yes, signora." My voice came from somewhere far away.

She left. I stood motionless, fingers still white-knuckled on the wood.

Africa. Return.

That night I pressed my forehead against the window glass in the servants' quarters, the coolness the only thing keeping me tethered. My reflection stared back. A woman I sometimes still didn't recognize. Not the girl who had run through Darfur forests. Not the slave who'd been renamed, beaten, sold.

Who was I now?

And who would I become if I stepped back onto that continent?

My breath fogged the glass. Through it, moonlight broke across the canal in pieces.

By dawn, I knew: I could not go back.

Sorella Maria found me in the chapel at the Catechumenate before the morning bell. I knelt in the last pew, gripping the wood so hard my palms ached.

"Bakhita?" Her voice was soft. "What troubles you?"

The words stuck. I had to force them out, one by one. "The family. They go to Africa. They say I—" My Italian failed. I started again in a mix of languages that probably made no sense. "I cannot. Return. Cannot be—" The word *slave* lodged in my throat like a stone.

She sat beside me. Waited.

"In Africa, I am..." I touched my wrist where the shackle scars still showed. "No protection. No rights. Here, at least..."

"Here, you have begun a new life," she said quietly. "In Christ."

My eyes burned. "Can I stay? Is this possible?"

"The law in Italy does not recognize slavery." She chose her words carefully. "If you choose to remain, the law should protect you. But the family considers you their... their property. They will not simply accept your choice."

"I know." My voice cracked.

"We can seek help. Legal counsel. The Canossian sisters have experience with such matters." She placed her hand over mine. "But you must be certain, Bakhita. This will not be easy. They will be angry. There may be threats."

I thought of Mimmina's small hand in mine. The guilt already spreading through my chest like a stain.

"I am certain," I whispered.

Was I? My pulse hammered against my throat, calling me a liar.

For two days, I moved through the Michieli household like a ghost walking through its own haunted house. Every time I looked at Mimmina, helping her dress, braiding her copper hair, wiping chocolate from her chin, the guilt pressed heavier.

She loved me. In her innocent, uncomplicated way, she loved me.

But Africa waited like an open grave.

On the third day, the mistress summoned me to her dressing room. I climbed the stairs slowly, my legs unsteady. When I entered, she was sorting gowns, holding silk up to the light.

"You've been distracted." She didn't look at me. "Are you unwell?"

Now. Say it now.

"Signora, I—" My mouth went dry. The words I'd practiced scattered. "I do not wish. To return. To Africa."

Her hands stilled on the fabric.

"I wish to remain. In Italy."

She turned, her expression caught between surprise and something harder. "Pardon?"

"I cannot return to Africa." My voice was steadier than I felt, but my hands were shaking. I hid them in my skirt.

A brittle laugh. "Cannot? Or will not?"

"Both, signora."

Her face flushed. "This is absurd. You are part of our household. You have duties. Obligations."

"In Africa—" I forced myself to meet her eyes, though everything in me screamed to look away. "In Africa, I could be sold. Again. Or worse."

"Preposterous. My husband would never do that."

"Not by your choice." The words came faster now, tumbling out before I lost courage. "By law. By custom. In Italy, I am a person. There, I am property."

"You have been listening to those sisters." Her voice sharp now. "They have filled your head with notions."

"They have taught me about God." My throat tightened. "And about dignity."

"Dignity!" She spat the word. Stepped closer. I fought the urge to step back. "Is this how you repay our kindness? Our care? After all we have done for you?"

The old shame rose, the habit of believing I deserved nothing, that every scrap of kindness was unearned. But behind it came something else. Something that tasted like anger.

"You have been good to me," I managed. My voice shook. "But I cannot return to a place where I might be enslaved again."

"And what of Mimmina?" She moved closer still, her perfume overwhelming. "She adores you. She needs you. You would abandon a child who loves you?"

The blade, cutting deep.

"I would stay if you remained in Italy," I offered, hating how my voice cracked.

The mistress turned away, shoulders rigid. "Get out. I will discuss this with my husband."

I fled.

That evening, a servant summoned me to Signor Michieli's study.

He sat behind his desk, hands steepled. The mistress stood by the window, a silhouette against the darkening sky. My heart hammered so loud I was certain they could hear it.

"My wife tells me you refuse to accompany us."

I stood as straight as I could manage, though my legs felt like water. "I desire to stay in Italy, signore."

"Why?"

The simple question. How could I explain the terror that gripped me at the thought of returning to the continent where I'd been hunted? Where I'd been nothing?

"I have found peace here." The words came out barely above a whisper. "And faith."

"You can practice your religion in Africa. We would not prevent it."

"It is not only that." I was trembling now, couldn't stop it. "In Africa, I would have no protection under the law. I could be taken from you. Sold. Enslaved again."

He waved a dismissive hand. "Unlikely. You would be under my protection."

"Until you leave." My voice stronger now, surprising me. "Or die."

His face darkened at my presumption. The mistress made a sharp sound of disapproval.

"I have spoken with the sisters at the Catechumenate," I continued, rushing before I lost courage completely. "They say they would allow me to stay there. While you are abroad."

"You have been making arrangements behind our backs?" The mistress turned from the window, voice like ice.

"I sought counsel, signora. Nothing is arranged without your permission."

Signor Michieli leaned back, studying me. The silence stretched. I couldn't breathe properly.

"You have changed, Bakhita."

I had. The realization settled in me. I was no longer the frightened girl bought in a Sudanese market. No longer the silent servant who accepted whatever fate was handed to her.

But my hands still shook. My pulse still raced. Courage, I was learning, didn't mean the absence of fear.

"The law in Italy—" I struggled to remember the Italian words Sorella Maria had taught me. "No slavery. The sisters told me. The law would..." I trailed off, unsure of the legal terms.

His expression hardened. "You are threatening legal action?"

"No, signore. I am asking..." My voice broke. I swallowed hard, tried again. "I am asking for your blessing. To remain here. To continue my religious instruction. To find my path."

"And if we refuse?" the mistress demanded.

I closed my eyes briefly. "Then I would refuse to board the ship." The words barely audible. "And the law would support me."

The silence that fell was crushing. I had never spoken to them this way, with authority, with certainty. It felt both terrifying and impossible, like standing at the edge of a great height.

The mistress made a sound of disgust. "This is outrageous. We should simply—"

"Enough." Signor Michieli raised his hand. Looked at me with something that might have been grudging respect, or might have been calculation. "This is irregular. Inconvenient."

"The sisters have offered to take me in," I repeated. "There would be no financial burden to you."

He exchanged a long look with his wife. An entire conversation passed between them, silent and impenetrable.

Finally, he sighed. "We will consider it. You may go."

I left on unsteady legs, aware that I had crossed a threshold from which there was no return.

Morning. The kitchen garden, where herbs grew in neat rows. Mimmina found me there, her small hand slipping into mine.

"Papa says you won't come with us to Africa."

Her voice was too quiet. Too careful.

I knelt, taking both her hands. "Your papa is right."

Her lower lip trembled. "Don't you love me anymore?"

Oh God.

"*Piccola mia.*" I pulled her close, breathed in the sweet scent of her hair. Honeysuckle soap and childhood. "I love you very much. But I cannot return to Africa."

"Why not?" Her fingers twisted in my apron. "Is it terrible there?"

How could I explain? This child who'd never known anything but privilege, security, love?

"For me, it would be."

"But you could stay with us. In our house. With me."

I stroked her cheek, trying to memorize the exact constellation of freckles across her nose. "Some paths we must walk alone, *piccola*. Even when it breaks our hearts."

"I hate Africa!" Her voice rose. "I won't go either!"

"Shh. You must go with your mama and papa. They need you."

"It won't be beautiful without you." She was crying now, hot tears soaking through my dress.

I held her. My own eyes remained dry. I couldn't afford to break, not here, not now. If I started crying, I might not be able to stop.

"When you see the moon at night," I whispered into her hair, "remember that I am looking at the same moon."

"Promise?"

"I promise."

Her father's voice called from the house, impatient. The mistress appeared in the doorway.

"Enough now. We'll miss our connection."

I pressed my lips to Mimmina's damp cheek one last time. "Be brave, *piccola mia*."

The mistress pried Mimmina's fingers from my skirt. The child was sobbing, reaching back for me. I stood frozen, arms empty, watching her be carried away.

The door closed.

I stood alone in the garden. A bee moved between lavender stalks, oblivious. The sun was warm on my shoulders. From somewhere distant came the sound of a canal boat, the call of the gondolier.

I had refused. After a lifetime of submission, I had drawn a line that could not be crossed.

Even for love.

Especially for love.

The price of freedom, I was learning, was not always paid in suffering. Sometimes it was paid in severance from the few pure things you'd managed to find in a broken world.

Three days later, the decision came. I was summoned again to Signor Michieli's study.

"We have spoken with the Mother Superior at the Catechumenate." His voice was clipped, formal. "Arrangements have been made. You will stay with the sisters while we are abroad."

Relief flooded through me so intensely my knees nearly buckled. I gripped the back of a chair.

"However—" His voice hardened. "You should understand that this arrangement is temporary. When we return from Africa, we will revisit the matter of your... status."

The threat implicit. They were not relinquishing their claim, merely postponing the battle.

"Thank you, signore." I bowed my head.

"Mimmina will be inconsolable." He sounded genuinely pained. "I hope you understand what you have done."

I understood. The guilt sat like a stone in my chest.

"That is all."

As I turned to leave, he spoke again.

"Bakhita."

I paused.

"What is it about Africa that terrifies you so?"

I turned to face him fully. Chose my words carefully.

"When I was a child, men came to our village. They took me from my family." My voice steady now, detached. "They chained me. Beat me. Marched me across deserts. Sold me many times before I was sixteen." I met his eyes. "That is the Africa I know, signore. Not the one in your business ledgers."

Something shifted in his expression. Not quite understanding, but perhaps the beginning of recognition that I existed beyond my function in his household.

"The past cannot be changed," he said quietly.

"No." I agreed. "But the future can."

Departure day arrived with slate-gray sky.

The household descended into controlled chaos—trunks being loaded, last-minute items packed, servants rushing to complete final tasks. I moved through it like a ghost watching its own life from a distance.

My belongings fit into a single cloth bundle. A change of clothes, the wooden rosary, a small book of prayers, a handkerchief embroidered by Mimmina. So little to show for a life.

The mistress was cool in our final interaction, instructing me on the transfer to the Catechumenate with brisk efficiency. If she felt betrayed, her face revealed nothing.

Mimmina was another matter.

She clung until the very last moment. I had to peel her fingers from my skirt, one by one.

"Promise you'll be here when we come back."

"I will be in Venice," I said carefully. Not a lie, not quite a promise. "And I will think of you every day."

"Every single day?"

"Every single day."

The gondola waited. Signor Michieli's impatient call from the water.

I knelt, pressed my lips to her forehead one final time. Her small body shook with sobs.

"Be brave."

Then the mistress led her away—down the steps, into the boat. Mimmina's pale face turned back, again and again, until the gondola rounded the corner and disappeared.

I stood on the *fondamenta* until the water was empty. Only then did I allow myself to acknowledge what I had done.

Another gondola waited to take me to the Catechumenate. I climbed in, bundle clutched to my chest. Rain began to fall, pattering against the roof, blurring Venice into watercolor.

The Catechumenate of the Canossian Sisters stood pale and fortress-like, its windows tall and narrow, courtyard enclosed by high walls thick with ivy.

The iron gates opened with a sigh.

Sorella Maria met me there. "Welcome, Bakhita. Come."

I followed her through the courtyard. A fountain played among roses just beginning to bloom. The sound of water on stone. Birdsong. From deeper within, the faint melody of women's voices raised in chant.

My room was small. A narrow bed with straw mattress, a wooden chair, a window facing east. A crucifix on the whitewashed wall.

"This is yours," Sorella Maria said, setting down my bundle. "For as long as you need it."

Yours. The word hung fragile in the air.

"We gather for the midday meal in one hour. You will hear the bell."

When she left, I stood motionless in the center of the room. The silence pressed against me, not the tense silence of a household awaiting a master's mood, but something deeper. It reminded me of the desert at night when the heat had bled away and the stars emerged.

I sat on the edge of the bed, half-expecting to be called to task for such presumption. When no admonishment came, I slowly lay back.

The ceiling was blank and white. No painted angels. No watching eyes. Just emptiness, waiting to be filled.

A strange feeling rose in my chest—part fear, part something I couldn't name.

I had refused to be taken back. I had claimed my right to remain.

But what came next?

The bell rang. I rose and followed its sound, not as one compelled, but as one who chooses.

The sisters ate in a long refectory with wooden tables and benches. Sunlight streamed through tall windows. I was shown a place among other women—some European, some not, all dressed simply, all with the same quiet attentiveness.

The meal began with prayer. Heads bowed, hands folded, voices joined in Latin I still didn't fully understand. Yet the rhythm washed over me like warm water.

"You do not need to work here as you did in the household," Sorella Maria explained afterward. "Though all share in tasks. You are here to learn."

"Learn?" The question slipped out.

"To read. To write. To know God." She smiled. "And perhaps, to know yourself."

Know myself. The words struck like flint on stone.

Who was I? The question had not seemed relevant for so many years. I had been what others made me—slave, servant, possession.

That night, unable to sleep, I crept to the chapel. Empty, lit only by the red lamp that burned eternally near the altar. I knelt in the last pew, watching the flame's reflection tremble on polished floor.

"What am I?" I whispered to the darkness. "Who?"

The silence answered with its own question: *Who did I wish to be?*

I thought of Africa, the continent that had birthed me and then betrayed me to chains. I thought of Sudan, where my family had lived, where perhaps they still searched the horizon. I thought of the deserts I had crossed, bleeding and afraid.

And I knew: I would never willingly return.

Not to please the Michielis. Not even to search for my lost family.

To return would be to surrender the selfhood I was just beginning to discover.

"I am Bakhita," I whispered to the empty chapel. "I am no one's property. I belong to myself and to God alone."

The words echoed in the vaulted space, bouncing from stone to stone until they seemed to come from everywhere at once.

A declaration.

A promise.

A beginning.

Days passed, then weeks. I fell into the rhythm of the convent, bells that marked hours, prayers that punctuated days, lessons that filled the spaces between.

I learned to read simple texts. I learned to write my name, the name I had been given, not the one I had lost. I learned stories of a God who had become man, who had suffered, who had died and risen.

Some days, I watched the sisters with fascination. They moved through the world with a certainty I had never known. Their eyes were clear, their hands steady. They laughed sometimes, a sound that startled me. They argued occasionally, voices firm but not cruel. They made mistakes and asked forgiveness.

They were women who owned themselves.

One afternoon in the garden, Sorella Fabretti joined me as I practiced sewing. She was older, with hands spotted by age and eyes the color of faded denim.

"You are quiet today." She took up her own needlework.

I nodded.

"Do you regret your decision? To refuse to return?"

The question surprised me. No one had asked this directly.

"No," I said, the certainty in my voice surprising even me. "I do not regret it."

"Even though it cost you the child's company?"

I stabbed my needle through linen. "I miss Mimmina. But I would miss myself more if I had gone."

She nodded, as if I had confirmed something she already knew.

"Africa is no longer my home," I continued slowly. "Perhaps it never truly was, once I was taken from my family. To return there would be to return to chains," I touched my wrist. "If not on my skin, then on my spirit."

"And here?" She asked. "What do you find here?"

I looked around the garden, orderly beds of herbs and vegetables, stone walls covered in climbing roses. Beyond them lay Venice, a city of water and light. And beyond that, a world I had only begun to glimpse.

"Possibility," I said finally. "Here, I find the possibility of becoming something I choose."

That night, I dreamed of the slave market in Khartoum. The familiar nightmare, stench of unwashed bodies, flies gathering, the crack of whips. But this time, something had changed.

In the dream, I saw myself from a distance, standing among the captives. And I realized I could see my face clearly now. Not the face of a victim, but of a woman who had refused captivity, who had claimed her right to be free.

I woke trembling, but not with fear.

Outside my window, the sky was beginning to lighten, stars fading.

I dressed and made my way to the chapel for morning prayers. The sisters were gathering, their veils creating a sea of black in the pale dawn. I took my place among them.

The Mother Superior began. "*In nomine Patris, et Filii, et Spiritus Sancti...*"

My hand moved to cross forehead, heart, and shoulders. A gesture that now felt natural as breathing.

A sister nearby smiled at me, a small acknowledgment.

Something settled inside me, a certainty, a recognition.

I was not Italian. I was not one of them. My skin, my history, my wounds set me apart.

But here, in this place of peace and prayer, I was not just the sum of what had been done to me.

I was becoming something else.

Someone else.

Someone who had refused to be taken back. Someone who had claimed her right to choose her own path, even when that choice severed ties to the only love she had known in this strange country.

I was becoming Bakhita, not the Bakhita named by slavers, but a woman who owned her own name and her own destiny.

Months passed. Summer came to Venice with heat that reminded me of home, though without the desert winds. The canals grew pungent. The convent courtyards burst with flowers—roses, jasmine, herbs whose names I learned: *basilico, rosmarino, salvia.*

One morning in August, a letter arrived from Africa.

The mistress wrote that they had established themselves in Suakin. The business prospered. Mimmina had grown two inches, had taken ill briefly but recovered. They would remain another year at least.

Of me, of my return—no mention. No demand that I prepare for their homecoming.

Perhaps they had accepted my decision. Perhaps they had simply decided I was not worth the trouble.

I read the letter three times. Sorella Maria watched my face.

"Are you disappointed?" she asked gently. "That they do not ask for your return?"

I considered the question, turning it over like a strange coin.

"No," I said firmly. "I am not."

That night, I dreamed again of the market. But this time, when I looked at my dream-self among the captives, I saw my face as it was now. Older, marked by suffering, yes.

But also by something else.

By dignity. By the first fragile shoots of hope. By the knowledge that I had refused to return to the land of my captivity.

And in that refusal, I had claimed my right to be free.

I woke with tears on my cheeks, but they were not tears of sorrow.

They were tears of recognition.

Of a woman who had finally found the courage to say no.

A woman who had chosen another path, another life, another possibility.

A woman who was, at last, becoming herself.

Chapter Nine

Autumn came with mist that clung to the convent walls and turned the canals to gray silk. In the kitchen, withered herbs hung from rafters, their scent sharp and medicinal. Baskets of wrinkled apples lined the storeroom shelves. The sisters prepared for All Saints' Day, polishing candlesticks until they gleamed.

I had been with them for six months.

The chapel smelled of beeswax and old incense. Stone floors held the chill even as spring approached. At night, I could hear the sisters' footsteps in the corridor above, soft, regular, a rhythm I was learning to find comfort in.

Six months of trying to understand who I was becoming.

The crucifix hung above the altar, larger than life, carved from dark wood that caught the candlelight. I could not stop looking at it. The ribs pressed against skin. The knees bent under the body's weight. Hands pierced, fingers curled.

And the face. Eyes raised to heaven, mouth parted as if caught between a plea and a sigh.

It was not the face of defeat.

I recognized it.

"You watch Him often."

I turned. Sorella Maria stood in the chapel doorway, her hands folded. The other sisters had gone to supper, but I had stayed.

"Who was He truly?" I asked, though I had heard the stories.

She sat beside me. "God who became man. Who chose to share our suffering."

"Why?" The word escaped before I could stop it. "If He is God, why not—" I gestured helplessly at the crucified figure. "Why not just save us? Without the blood?"

She was quiet for a long moment. "Love," she said finally. "He could not love us from a distance."

Love. The word sat strange in my mouth.

"Did it hurt Him?" My eyes traced the carved wounds. "As much as it would hurt a person?"

"Yes. Perhaps more."

My hand moved to my arm, where scars still raised the skin in ridged patterns. I thought of the branding iron. The blade cutting decorative patterns into my chest as if my body were pottery to be carved.

Christ had been scarred too.

That night, I dreamed of the cross. Not the polished chapel crucifix, but rough wood on a barren hill. A man hung there, blood running hot and real, breath coming in ragged gasps.

He turned His face toward me.

Anche io, He whispered. *Me too.*

I woke with tears on my face, heart hammering. Pre-dawn darkness pressed against my window. I rose, knelt beside my bed, hands clasped awkwardly.

I had no words.

But somehow, on that gray morning, I felt something I had no name for.

"Bakhita." Sorella Fabretti found me after breakfast. "Father Illuminato will begin catechism today."

I followed her to a small room where other women waited. Young Italian novices preparing for vows. A Greek woman. Two Armenians. A Moroccan girl with hennaed hands.

Father Illuminato was older than I expected. White hair framed his bald head; hands spotted with age. But when he spoke, his voice filled the room.

"We begin at the beginning. *In principio erat Verbum.* In the beginning was the Word."

He spoke of creation. Light separated from darkness. Waters gathered, land revealed. Creatures formed from dust and breath. A garden. Innocence. A fall.

I listened, trying to fit these stories against fragments I remembered from childhood. The great river that birthed the world. Spirits in baobab trees. The first people emerging from a crack in the earth.

Different words. Same longing to understand where we came from.

"Next week," Father Illuminato said as we departed, "we will speak of sin."

Sin. The word tasted bitter, like unripe fruit.

That afternoon in the kitchen, peeling potatoes for soup, my knife slipped. A thin red line opened across my palm, blood welling in perfect beads.

Sister Angelica clucked her tongue, wrapped my hand in clean cloth. "Press hard," she instructed, guiding my fingers. "It will stop soon."

Press hard. It will stop soon.

The words echoed. Different voice. An older woman, what was her name? Darkness. The smell of herbs. My back on fire from the cane. Gentle hands in that storage room where I slept. *Press hard, child. It will stop.*

"Bakhita?" Sister Angelica's face swam before me.

I was in the convent kitchen. Not that dark room. Not that other life.

"I remembered something," I whispered.

She retrieved the potato that had fallen from my hand. "The body remembers what the mind tries to forget. It is not a sin to have suffered, child."

But was it a sin to still be suffering? Even here, even safe, still carrying those wounds?

The catechism lessons continued through winter. Prophets who foretold Christ's coming. Mary who bore Him. Apostles who followed Him. Miracles, water to wine, sight to the blind, the dead raised.

Always, we returned to the cross.

"Why did He have to die?" the Greek woman asked one day, her face troubled. "Could He not save us another way?"

Father Illuminato sighed. "He could have. But He chose to enter fully into our condition. To experience abandonment. Betrayal. Physical agony."

To know what it is to be a slave, I thought, though I did not speak.

During the lessons, memories returned. Fragments, sharp as broken glass.

My father carrying me on his shoulders, his hands strong around my ankles.

My sister teaching me to grind grain, showing me how to test its fineness.

The raid. Shouting, smoke, a hand clamped over my mouth.

The first time I was sold. Standing naked before strangers who inspected my teeth, my limbs.

The branding.

This memory came during evening prayers. The sisters chanted the Magnificat, voices rising like incense. *My soul magnifies the Lord, and my spirit rejoices in God my Savior...*

And suddenly I was there. Dim room smelling of charcoal and fear. Bowls of flour and salt. The sharp razor. Being held down, weight crushing the breath from my lungs. Metal pressed against skin.

The world went white with pain.

I made a sound. Sorella Maria turned, her chant faltering. She saw my face, was beside me in an instant.

"Come." She guided me from the chapel into the cool corridor. "Breathe, Bakhita. You are here, not there."

In the kitchen, she pressed wine into my hands. "Drink."

It burned down my throat, anchoring me to the present.

"The memories," I managed.

She nodded. "As you open your heart to God, old wounds may reopen before they heal."

"Will they ever heal?" The question tore from me. "Will I ever be free?"

She took my hands, my dark fingers against her pale ones. "I cannot promise you will forget. But one day, the memories will lose their power to wound. They will be scars, not open sores."

I thought of Christ's scars. Thomas had placed his fingers in those wounds, finding faith in their reality.

Perhaps scars could be sacred.

Spring approached. Crocuses pushed through soil, buds swelled on fruit trees, birds returned to nests. Life reasserting itself.

I had been at the Catechumenate nearly a year. My Italian had improved. I could read simple texts, follow the liturgy, make the sign of the cross at appropriate moments.

But more than these external changes, something within had shifted.

One morning, a letter arrived.

I was helping Sister Angelica in the kitchen when Sorella Maria appeared in the doorway. Her face was carefully composed.

"Bakhita. Come with me, please."

My hands stilled on the dough I was kneading. That tone. I knew that tone.

In the small parlor, she handed me the letter. The Michieli family seal pressed into wax.

My hands shook as I unfolded it. The Italian words swam before my eyes. I caught fragments: *...conclude our business... ...return to Venice... ...three months' time... ...expect you to resume...*

Three months.

They were coming back.

"What will you do?" Sorella Maria asked gently.

I stared at the letter. Three months to decide who I would be.

That night, sleep would not come. I rose and made my way to the chapel. Empty except for the red lamp burning near the altar. I knelt, watching the flame's reflection tremble on stone.

"What do You want from me?" I whispered to the darkness. "What am I supposed to do?"

The Christ on the cross did not answer. He hung there, suffering, silent.

I thought of returning to the Michieli household. Sleeping in the servants' quarters. Caring for Mimmina. She would be taller now, more grown. The mistress's cool commands. The careful navigation of a world where I existed at someone else's pleasure.

And I thought of staying. Of the baptism I had begun to want. Of belonging to something beyond any human master.

"He chose this," I said to the crucified figure. My voice echoed in the empty chapel. "But I didn't choose."

My throat closed. I tried again.

"What does that mean? That He chose and I didn't?"

The silence pressed back.

I rose and moved closer to the altar, stood directly beneath the cross. From here, I could see details invisible from the pews. The grain of the wood. The way the carver had rendered each thorn in the crown. The gash in the side, deep and terrible.

"Were You afraid?" I asked. "When they came for You. When they put the nails through your body?" I touched my own palm, feeling the echo of pain that had never happened there. "Were You afraid?"

Of course He was, something whispered in my mind. *He sweat blood in the garden. He begged for the cup to pass.*

He was afraid. And He chose it anyway.

I stood there until my legs ached, until the sky outside began to lighten from black to gray. When I finally left the chapel, I had not found an answer.

But I had found a question worth asking.

The next day, during catechism, I could not concentrate. Father Illuminato spoke of the resurrection, but my mind turned over and over the problem of choice.

"You are distracted," he observed, his hawk-sharp eyes on me.

The other women glanced my way. I felt heat rise to my face.

"The Michieli family is returning," I said. "In three months."

He nodded slowly. "I see."

"I do not know what to do."

"What do you wish to do?"

The question caught me off guard. No one had ever asked me that before. What I wished.

"I wish..." My voice faltered. "I wish to stay. To be baptized. But—"

"But?"

"They will expect me to return with them. To Africa."

"And if you refuse?"

"I do not know what will happen." The uncertainty terrified me. "The law may protect me. Or it may not. They may accept my decision. Or they may not."

Father Illuminato was quiet for a moment. Then he gestured toward the window, where beyond lay the chapel and its crucifix. "He remained. That is faith."

My hand moved unconsciously to the scars on my arm. *He remained.*

That afternoon, I found myself in the garden with Sorella Fabretti. We were tying up bean plants, our fingers working in companionable silence. The spring sun was warm on my shoulders, the smell of turned earth all around.

"Do you regret taking your vows?" I asked suddenly.

She glanced at me, surprised. "Why do you ask?"

"You gave up your freedom. Your choice of where to go, what to do. You belong to the Order now."

She smiled, her old face creasing. "I belong to God, child. That is a different thing entirely from belonging to any human master."

"But how do you know?" I pressed. "How do you know it is worth it? The sacrifice?"

She tied off a vine, her spotted hands sure and steady. "I do not always know. Some days I doubt. Some days I long for the life I might have had." She met my eyes. "But those days pass. And what remains is the knowing that I am where I am meant to be."

"Even without certainty?"

"Especially without certainty. Faith that requires certainty is not faith at all."

That night, I dreamed again.

I stood at the foot of an empty tomb. A great stone rolled away from the dark opening. I expected to find death inside—decay, stillness, ending.

Instead, light poured out.

It touched my feet first. Hot, unbearably hot, like desert sand at midday. I tried to step back, but it rose to my ankles, my calves. Where it touched the whip scars on my legs, my skin burned. Not the burn of the branding iron, but different. Like infection draining from a wound.

I gasped, fell to my knees. The light reached the scarification on my chest. I opened my mouth to scream.

And tasted honey.

Sweet, golden, impossible. The light filled my mouth, my throat, flooded through me. Where it went, the burning eased. The scars remained. I could feel them beneath my skin. But they were quiet now. Resting.

A voice spoke. Not in Italian or Arabic or the language of my childhood, but in a tongue my soul somehow recognized.

Daughter. I have called you by name. You are Mine.

I woke gasping, hands pressed to my chest. Outside, dawn was breaking, pale and new.

I rose and went to the small mirror in the washroom. My reflection looked back, dark skin, tightly coiled hair, eyes that had seen too much.

The same features that had been mine since birth.

But something was different now.

For the first time in many years, I recognized the person looking back.

Three months became two and a half. Then two.

I moved through my days in strange suspension, helping in the kitchen, attending prayers, while inside, a battle raged.

One morning, I entered the chapel and found I was not alone. A young woman knelt in the front pew, shoulders shaking with sobs.

I hesitated, then approached. "Sister?"

She looked up. It was Maria, one of the Italian novices from catechism. Her face was blotchy, eyes swollen.

"I cannot do it," she gasped. "I thought I could, but I cannot."

I sat beside her. "Do what?"

"Take my vows next month." She twisted her hands in her lap. "Everyone expects it. My family has already told everyone. But I—" She broke off, fresh tears spilling. "I do not want this life. I want to marry Pietro from my village. I want children. I want..."

"Freedom," I said quietly.

She nodded miserably. "But how can I tell them? After everything? After they have paid for my dowry here, after all the preparations?"

I looked up at the crucifix. Christ hanging there, wounds open, choosing.

"What will happen if you take vows you do not mean?" I asked.

"I will be miserable," she whispered. "And it will be a lie."

"Then you must tell them."

"But they will be so angry. So disappointed."

I took her hand. "Yes. They will. But Maria—" I turned her face toward mine. "You will still be alive. Angry and disappointed, but alive and true. Is that not worth something?"

She stared at me. "How can you say that so certainly?"

I thought of the years I had been silent. The years I had obeyed without question, bent myself into whatever shape others required. The slow death of the self that came from always choosing safety over truth.

"Because I know what it costs to live a lie," I said. "And the price is too high."

She left with her tears dried, shoulders straighter. Two days later, I saw Maria in the refectory. Her eyes were red, but her shoulders were straight. She had spoken her truth. Whatever came next, she would face it free.

That same afternoon, I found Mother Superior in her small office.

She looked up from her correspondence, eyebrows raised. I rarely sought her out.

"I wish to be baptized," I said. The words emerged clear, certain. "Before the Michielis return."

She studied me with her bird-of-prey gaze. "This is not a decision to be made lightly. Or in haste."

"I am not making it in haste." My voice was steady. "I have been making it for a year. Every day, with every prayer, every lesson, every moment I have stood before the cross."

"The path of faith is not an easy one," she warned.

"I know." I thought of the crucifix. The wounds. The choice. "But I have found something here I cannot name and cannot lose."

She was silent for a long moment. Then, to my surprise, she smiled. It transformed her stern face into something almost gentle.

"Very well. I will speak with Father Illuminato." She paused. "And the Michielis? When they return?"

"I do not know what will happen." I met her eyes. "But I know that I cannot go back to Africa. I cannot return to being property. Whatever that costs."

She nodded slowly. "You have grown strong, Bakhita."

"No," I said. "I am still afraid. But I am learning that being afraid and being brave are not opposites."

The baptism was arranged for two weeks hence. Father Illuminato began my final preparation, intensive instruction, the sacrament of confession, the learning of specific prayers and responses.

During these days, everything felt both more vivid and more fragile. The taste of bread at meals. The sound of sisters laughing in the garden. The weight of rosary beads in my hands. The cool press of stone floor against my knees during prayer.

I was counting down to something. A death and a birth.

One evening, I stood again before the crucifix. The chapel was empty, the red lamp burning steady. Candlelight flickered across the carved wood, making shadows dance.

"I do not know if I understand You yet," I whispered to the figure on the cross. "I do not know if Your wounds can heal mine, or if that is even how it works."

The carved face gazed upward, silent.

"But I want to find out." My voice grew stronger. "I want to belong to something that cannot be bought or sold. I want to have a name that no one can take from me."

The Christ hung there, suffering and surrendered.

And somehow, in His wounds, I saw my own reflection.

Not the wounds themselves. Those I would carry always. But in the way He bore them. Not with shame or defeat, but with a strange kind of triumph.

This is what was done to Me, those wounds proclaimed. *But it is not who I am.*

I touched my scarred arm. Traced the ridged patterns on my chest beneath my dress.

This is what was done to me. But it is not who I am.

The tears came then, not of sorrow, but of something like relief. Like a burden I had carried so long I'd forgotten it was there, finally being set down.

I knelt. Not in the posture of a slave before a master, but in the posture of a child before a father. A daughter before the one who had called her by name.

"I am Yours," I whispered. "Whatever that means. However this ends. I am Yours."

The red lamp flickered. The chapel held its breath.

And in the silence, I felt something that might have been an answer. Or might have been my own heart, learning at last to beat without permission.

The night before my baptism, I stood at my window watching moonlight silver the canal below.

Tomorrow, I would be baptized. Tomorrow, I would take the name Josephine. Tomorrow, I would belong to God in a way no human could claim.

And in six weeks, the Michielis would return.

I did not know what would happen then. Whether the law would protect me. Whether my faith would be tested immediately or granted time to root.

But the man on the cross had shown me something: He had chosen. Even knowing the outcome, even feeling the fear, He had chosen.

And in choosing, He had transformed suffering from something that happened *to* Him into something He moved *through*.

Tomorrow, I would choose too.

From somewhere in the convent, a bell chimed the hour. I stood at my window and waited for the dawn.

Chapter Ten

The day of my baptism dawned cold and bright.

January sunlight spilled through the chapel windows, casting pools of gold across the stone floor. Outside, Venice lay wrapped in winter stillness, the canals dark mirrors beneath a sky so blue it hurt to look at it. Inside, candles burned against the chill, their flames dancing in glass cups.

I had spent the night in vigil, as was the custom. Alone in the chapel, kneeling before the altar, I whispered the prayers I now knew by heart , the Our Father, the Hail Mary, the Apostles' Creed. Words that had once been foreign now worn smooth by use, like river stones in the palm.

Three months of preparation had led to this morning. Three months of instruction from Father Illuminato, of learning the mysteries of faith, of examining my conscience with an intensity that sometimes left me breathless.

When the first bell rang, Sorella Maria came to fetch me. She carried a bundle of white cloth.

"It is time," she said, her voice soft. "Are you ready?"

I nodded, though ready seemed too small a word. I stood at the edge of something vast, waters both terrifying and welcoming.

The sisters had prepared a small room near the chapel. The white gown was simply cut but beautifully made, with tiny stitches that spoke of careful hands. I slipped it over my head, the cool linen settling against my skin.

"This symbolizes purity," Sorella Maria said, adjusting the folds. "Not the purity of one who has never known sin, but the purity of one who has been cleansed."

She placed a wreath of winter jasmine on my head, the small white blossoms stark against my dark hair. Their scent was subtle but piercing, a sweetness cutting through the chapel's usual perfume of incense and beeswax.

"Every baptism is a wedding," she continued, her voice catching slightly. "The soul joined to Christ."

I looked at my reflection in the small mirror on the wall. The woman gazing back was a stranger — draped in white, crowned with flowers, eyes steady. I raised one hand and pressed my fingertips to the glass, as though testing whether she was real. She looked nothing like the girl who had arrived at the convent more than a year ago, shoulders drawn in, moving along the edges of rooms as though she had no right to the center.

And yet she was more truly me than I had been in years.

I lowered my hand. My fingers left a brief fog on the glass, then cleared.

"I have chosen my name," I said.

Sorella Maria nodded, unsurprised. Those preparing for baptism could select a Christian name, a new identity to mark their rebirth in faith.

"Josephine," I said. "Josephine Margaret."

"Why these?" she asked, not questioning but curious.

"Joseph was the protector of the Holy Family. He guided them to safety in a foreign land. And Margaret, was she not a pearl of great price? Hidden, then discovered, then treasured."

I said nothing of the nights those names had come to me, arriving in the dark without explanation and staying. Some things did not require accounting for. They simply were.

"And your surname?" she asked.

I hesitated. The question had troubled me. I had no family name to claim, no lineage I could remember with certainty.

"Bakhita," I said finally. "I will keep Bakhita."

Her eyebrows rose. "The name given by your captors?"

"It means fortunate one. They meant it in mockery." I touched the jasmine wreath, its petals cool against my fingers. "Now I choose to make it true."

A rare full smile transformed her usually composed features. "Josephine Margaret Bakhita," she repeated. "It is a good name."

The second bell rang.

The chapel had been transformed. White cloths draped the altar. Candles burned in every sconce. The baptismal font, usually tucked in a side alcove, had been moved to the center before the altar. Its silver basin gleamed, the water catching and fracturing the candlelight into a thousand dancing fragments.

The sisters had gathered in a semicircle around the font, their faces solemn but their eyes warm. Father Illuminato stood before them in white vestments embroidered with gold thread. Beside him stood the Cardinal from Venice, his robes the color of wine, rich and somber against the surrounding white.

I walked the center aisle alone, my bare feet silent on the stone floor. The weight of what I was leaving lay behind me with each step, not forgotten, but changed. The scars on my body no longer spoke only of cruelty endured. They marked a journey completed, a wilderness crossed.

At the font, I knelt.

Father Illuminato's voice rose, filling the chapel with ancient words.

"Do you reject Satan and all his works?"

"I do." My voice was clear.

"Do you believe in God the Father Almighty, creator of heaven and earth?"

"I do."

"Do you believe in Jesus Christ, His only Son, our Lord, who was born and suffered for us?"

"I do."

"Do you believe in the Holy Spirit, the Holy Catholic Church, the communion of saints, the forgiveness of sins, the resurrection of the body, and life everlasting?"

"I do."

The water came, cool against my forehead, streaming down my face, across the scars on my collarbone, dripping from my chin onto the stone floor. Then the chrism oil, pressed into my brow in the sign of the cross, its resinous warmth spreading outward from the mark. Then the weight of hands upon my head, blessing, confirming, claiming.

And through it all, a presence, invisible, unhurried, that I had known before. The one from the cross. The one from the empty tomb. The one who had called me by name when all other names had been stolen.

"Josephine Margaret Bakhita," pronounced Father Illuminato. "You have been washed clean. You have been sealed with the gift of the Holy Spirit. You have been marked as Christ's own forever."

A single breath of silence.

Then the sisters' voices rose together, an Amen that seemed to vibrate in the very stone of the chapel.

Afterward, there was a small celebration in the refectory. Sweet bread and wine were served, an indulgence rare in the ascetic life of the community. The Cardinal spoke briefly, his Latin flowing into Italian as he welcomed me into the family of the Church.

"Every baptism is a miracle," he said, his voice resonant in the vaulted space. "But some speak more clearly than others of the transforming power of Christ's love."

His eyes met mine across the table. "You have traveled far, Josephine. Not only from Africa to Italy, but from bondage to something else altogether."

Freedom. The word formed itself without being spoken. Was I free? Legally, I remained the property of the Michielis, though they were an ocean away. Yet something had shifted. Not the chains at my wrists, which had been gone for years, but something that had persisted long after the iron was removed.

Later, as the celebrations wound down and the sisters returned to their duties, I sought the garden. Despite the winter chill, I needed air, space enough to hold what had happened.

The garden was bare, its trees stripped to elegant skeletons against the sky, its beds tucked under straw against the cold. Every bare branch held its shape against the grey, patient, unashamed of what it had shed.

I sat on a stone bench. I had exchanged the baptismal gown for my simple dress, but kept the jasmine wreath. Its fragrance had faded, the circle still intact.

"Josephine."

Sorella Fabretti approached, her black veil moving in the winter breeze. She sat beside me, her aged hands clasped in her lap.

"How do you feel?" she asked.

I had spent years knowing precisely where I stood in every room I entered, what I was permitted, what was forbidden, where the danger lay. Here I knew none of those things, and the not-knowing did not frighten me. That was new. That was what had changed.

"Complete," I said. "For the first time since the forest, I feel complete."

She nodded. "Baptism does not erase the past. It redeems it."

I turned the word around in my mind. Not the wiping away of what had been, but the transformation of it. A garden takes in death, fallen leaves, withered blooms, and turns it to nourishment.

"The sisters have given me this," I said, drawing a small silver cross on a chain from my pocket. "My first gift as Josephine."

"May I?" She held out her hand.

I placed the cross in her palm. She turned it over, examining the simple design. Christ's figure rendered in minimal lines, more suggestion than detail.

"In the early Church," she said, "they did not depict Christ upon the cross. They showed it empty, or adorned with jewels. The suffering was too raw, too recent. It took centuries before Christians could look directly at what had been done."

She returned the cross to me. I closed my fingers around it, feeling its edges press into my palm.

"Why look at it at all?" I asked. "Why not remember only the resurrection?"

Her smile was gentle but carried something sad. "Because to look away from suffering is to look away from much of what it means to be human. Christ came not to call us out of our humanity, but deeper into it."

I fastened the chain around my neck and felt the cross settle against my breastbone.

That evening, after vespers, I wrote in the small journal Sorella Maria had given me as a baptismal gift. My letters were still uneven; each word formed with effort.

Today I am Josephine. The girl before is still me. The slave. The servant. All of them. But not only them. Not anymore.

I set the pen down and touched the scars on my abdomen through the thin fabric of my nightdress, feeling their raised patterns. For so long they had been marks of violation. They were becoming something else. A testament, a map of where I had been and how far I had traveled.

That night I dreamed of a table set for a feast, bread and wine and fruits of every kind arranged across its length. Around it sat people of all nations, faces dark as night and pale as dawn, eyes of every shape and color, hands bearing the marks of every kind of labor and suffering. At the head of the table stood the man from the cross, no longer bleeding but still bearing the scars in his hands and feet and side. He broke bread, and as he did, his eyes found mine.

"Josephine," he said, and my new name in his mouth became a sacrament.

I woke with the taste of bread on my tongue and salt on my cheeks. Tears shed not in sorrow but in recognition.

The days following my baptism took on a different quality, sharper, clearer, as though a veil had been lifted from my senses. I moved through the familiar routines of convent life, prayer, work, study, reflection, but with a new awareness of their weight and meaning.

Scrubbing the chapel floor was no longer a task assigned, but an act given freely. Preparing the evening meal was not servitude. Studying the scriptures was not rote memorization required of a servant, but the exploration of a story in which I now had a place.

One afternoon, helping Sister Angelica turn the winter soil for spring planting, I felt her pause in her work and look at me.

"You're different," she said.

I glanced up, brushing dirt from my hands. "Am I?"

"You stand straighter. You look people in the eye." A brief pause. "You laugh."

I had not noticed these changes, these small rebellions against the posture that had been beaten into me. They had come on their own, the way water finds its level.

"Is that bad?" I asked.

Her laugh was warm. "It is very good. Baptism should not make us something other than ourselves. It should make us more fully ourselves, as God intended."

A letter arrived from Africa that same week. The Michielis wrote that their business was prospering and that they had decided to remain another year. Mimmina had grown tall and was learning Arabic. They inquired after my welfare, instructed the sisters to continue my education, and enclosed funds for my keep.

Not once did they ask what I wished.

I read the letter twice, then set it face-down on my writing table. The words that troubled me were not harsh ones. They were ordinary, polite, even. But they had been written by people who looked to Venice and still saw the same Bakhita who had left it. A girl whose days were arranged by others, whose place in any room was decided before she entered it. They had not seen me walk the center aisle. They had not heard my voice fill the chapel.

They did not know yet who I had become.

I covered the letter with my journal and did not read it again.

That night I dreamed of Africa. Not the Africa of slave markets and branding houses, but the Africa of my earliest years. The village with its circle of huts, the fields beyond, the great trees standing against the horizon like sentinels.

I walked through the village, but no one saw me. I called out and no one heard. Then a young girl appeared before me, perhaps nine or ten years old, with bright eyes and quick hands. It took a moment to understand I was looking at myself, as I had been before the raid. She looked at me directly, unafraid.

"Who are you?" she asked, in the language of my childhood.

"Josephine," I said. "Josephine Margaret Bakhita."

She tilted her head. "That is not the name our mother gave you."

"No. But it is the name I have chosen."

She stepped closer and reached out to touch the scars on my arms, her small fingers careful. "They hurt you," she said. Not a question.

"Yes. Very much."

"Why?" In that single word lay everything I had carried through years of bondage.

I knelt before her and took her hands in mine. "I do not know why," I said. "But I know who I have become because of it."

She studied me with the direct gaze of a child who has not yet learned to look away from difficult things.

"Are you free now?"

"I am becoming free," I said.

She reached up and touched my face, her palm warm against my cheek.

"Remember me," she said.

"Always," I promised.

I woke with the word still on my lips, her warmth still against my skin. Across the rooftops, the bell of San Marco struck the early hour, its voice rolling out over the city and dissolving into the cold air.

I, Josephine Margaret Bakhita, rose and went out to meet the day.

Chapter Eleven

The letter arrived on the Feast of the Annunciation when spring had just begun to touch Venice with tentative fingers. Buds swelled on the convent's apple trees, and sparrows gathered twigs for nests beneath the eaves. The air smelled of damp stone and possibility.

Nearly three months had passed since my baptism. Three months of living into my new name, of learning to read the Gospels in halting Italian, of finding my place within the rhythm of the convent. Three months of freedom I had never known before, not of body, perhaps, but of spirit.

The letter was a calling card of sorts. A single page delivered by a servant boy that morning, informing the sisters that the Michielis had returned to Venice and would call within the hour. By the time Sorella Maria came to find me in the garden, they were already waiting in the parlor.

Sorella Maria found me where I was turning the soil for the spring planting, my hands black with earth, sweat dampening my collar despite the cool March air.

"Josephine," she said, and something in her voice made me straighten, the trowel still in my hand. "A messenger has come. The Michielis. They have returned to Venice and are here now."

The name fell between us. For a moment I could not speak. In the months since my baptism, the Michielis had receded in my mind, not forgotten, but distant, like figures in a story told long ago.

"They wish to see you," Sorella Maria continued, her voice gentle but firm. "They have come to collect you."

Collect. How easily the language of ownership returned, even from the lips of one who had taught me dignity.

I set the trowel down with care. "When?"

"They are waiting in the parlor now."

I looked down at my soil-stained dress, my rough apron, my bare feet caked with garden earth.

"I should change," I said. The words came without thought, the old reflex of the servant.

Sorella Maria's hand closed on my arm. "Josephine. You do not have to go with them."

I stared at her. "What do you mean?"

"Italian law does not recognize slavery. If you choose to remain here, there may be a way."

Choose. The word landed with a weight I could not measure. Throughout my life, choices had belonged to others. The notion that I might refuse to return was as foreign to me as the concept of flight would be to a fish.

"Is such a thing possible?" I asked.

Her eyes were steady on mine. "I do not know. But Cardinal Lavigerie has been advocating against the slave trade. There are those who would support your case. It would not be easy, but it may be possible."

"They are waiting," I said. I could not hold the implications of what she suggested. Not yet. "I should not keep them waiting."

She released my arm. "Change if you wish. I will tell them you will come shortly."

In my small room, I stripped off my gardening clothes. I washed in the basin, watching the water darken with the soil of the convent garden, this place that had become the first ground in years I had thought of as mine. I dressed in the simple blue dress given to me at Christmas, smoothed my hair, and fastened the silver cross at my throat.

In the mirror, a woman looked back, perhaps twenty years old, though I could not be certain of my age. My face had filled out during my time with the sisters. My eyes held a steadiness that had not been there before.

I pressed two fingers briefly to the glass, as I had done on the morning of my baptism.

"Josephine Margaret Bakhita," I said to her. "Remember who you are."

The walk to the convent parlor was the longest I had ever made. Each step carried me further from the self I had discovered and closer to the self I had been. The silent servant, the obedient slave, the thing owned rather than the woman choosing.

They were waiting in the formal receiving room, Signor Michieli, Signora Turina, and Mimmina, now eleven years old and inches taller than when I had last seen her. They turned as I entered, the father with polite distance, the mother with impatience already arranged across her features, the child with unrestrained joy.

"Bakhita!" Mimmina cried, rushing toward me with arms outstretched. I caught her, the familiarity of her slight weight against me a shock after so long.

"You have grown," I said, the words inadequate.

"And you look different," she replied, stepping back to examine me with a child's frank curiosity.

"Mimmina, let her breathe." The signora's voice was as I remembered, cultured, controlled, expecting obedience without needing to demand it. "Bakhita. You are well?"

"Yes, signora." The old patterns of servitude rose in me before I could stop them. "I am well."

"Good. We have returned earlier than expected. The climate in Sudan did not agree with Mimmina, and the business no longer requires our presence." She gestured. "We leave for the house in Zianigo tomorrow. You will come with us, of course. Mimmina has missed you terribly."

Not a question. An arrangement already made, the way one arranges luggage or books passage on a vessel. I looked at Signor Michieli, whose face stayed impassive, then at Mimmina, whose eyes shone.

"I..." The words stopped in my throat.

Mother Superior entered then, her tall figure commanding attention without effort. "Signor, Signora Michieli," she said, inclining her head. "Welcome back to Venice. I trust your time in Africa was productive."

"Thank you, Reverend Mother," replied the signor. "We are grateful for your care of our servant in our absence."

"Josephine has been an exemplary member of our community," she said, and I noted her use of my baptismal name. "She has been received into the Catholic faith and has shown a remarkable aptitude for its practice."

The signora's eyebrows rose. "Baptized? Well, that is all very well, but it changes nothing. She remains in our employ and we have need of her services."

Mother Superior's face stayed serene, but I saw the slight stiffening at her shoulders. "Perhaps we might discuss this further. The situation is more complex than it appears."

"There is nothing to discuss." The signora's patience was thinning visibly. "The girl is ours. We have papers from the Italian consul in Khartoum confirming our ownership."

"Italian law does not recognize such ownership," said Mother Superior, her voice gentle but unyielding. "And Josephine has expressed a desire to remain with us."

The silence that followed pressed against the walls of the room. Every gaze turned to me: the sisters' steadiness, the signora's disbelief, Mimmina's confusion.

"Is this true?" Signor Michieli asked, addressing me directly for perhaps the first time in our acquaintance. "You wish to stay here with the sisters?"

My mouth was dry. To refuse them was to sever my connection not just to the Michielis, but to the only life I had known since arriving in Italy. To return was to surrender the self I had discovered, the name I had chosen, the dignity I had claimed.

"Yes," I said. The word barely reached the air. Then, steadier: "Yes. I wish to remain."

Mimmina's face crumpled. "But you're coming home with us. You promised you'd always take care of me!"

I had made no such promise. Yet she believed it, and in her belief lay the power to undo me. I knelt to meet her at eye level. Her tears had already begun.

"Mimmina," I said. "I care for you very much. But I have found something here that I cannot leave."

"What?" Tears spilled down her cheeks. "What is more important than us?"

I took her hands in mine and held them, saying nothing for a moment. There were no words a child of eleven could receive. There was only the grip of my hands on hers, and the truth I could not yet give her.

"My future," I said finally.

The signora's laugh was a short, cold sound. "Your future? You are a servant, Bakhita. A fortunate one. We have treated you well, given you far more than most in your position could expect. But your place is with us."

I rose to my feet. "My name is Josephine."

The signora's eyes narrowed. "This is absurd. Come. You may gather your things and meet us at the house tomorrow morning."

Mother Superior stepped forward, placing herself quietly between me and the Michielis. "I am afraid it is not so simple, signora. If Josephine chooses to remain, and if Italian law does not recognize your claim, we have reached an impasse that cannot be resolved by force."

Signor Michieli, who had been watching with growing discomfort, finally spoke. "What do you propose?"

"The law must decide," said Mother Superior. "Until then, Josephine remains here, under our protection."

"This is outrageous," said the signora. Color had risen in her cheeks. "We paid good money for the girl. We have invested years in her care. She belongs to us."

"No person can belong to another under the laws of this land," said Mother Superior, her voice still calm but now carrying an edge that did not bend. "The question will be settled by the courts, not by our desires, nor yours, nor even Josephine's."

Mimmina wept in earnest now, clinging to her mother's skirts. The signora stroked her hair without looking at her, her gaze fixed on me.

"You will regret this ingratitude," she said, each word placed with precision. "When the judge hears how we rescued you, clothed you, fed you, entrusted our own child to your care, do you truly believe he will side with you over us?"

I did not answer. What could I say that would not become exactly the ingratitude she accused me of? They had been kinder than most. They had not beaten me, not starved me, not subjected me to the worst I had known in Africa. Was it wrong to want more than the absence of cruelty?

Signor Michieli placed a restraining hand on his wife's arm. "We shall see what the law has to say." He bowed slightly to Mother Superior. "You will hear from our lawyer tomorrow."

They left in a rustle of silk and French perfume, Mimmina's sobs fading down the corridor. When the door closed, my legs gave way beneath me and I sank into the nearest chair, my hands shaking against my knees.

"What have I done?" I whispered.

Mother Superior sat beside me, her face grave but kind. "You have claimed your God-given right to freedom, child. It will not be an easy path. But you will not walk it alone."

Sleep would not come that night. I stood at my window, watching the moon lay silver across the canal. I worked in my mind the same ground I had already covered in the parlor, asking the same questions, finding no new answers. Near dawn I stopped and knelt beside the bed instead.

Not the formal prayers I had learned. A palm pressed flat against the coverlet. A face turned upward. A silence that asked everything and said nothing.

What came was not a voice. It was a memory.

The water cool against my forehead. The weight of hands upon my head. Father Illuminato's voice filling the chapel's stillness: *Josephine Margaret Bakhita. You have been marked as Christ's own forever.*

I could not go back. The die was cast.

Two days later the summons came. The Michielis had engaged a lawyer, and the case would be heard before a magistrate the following week. Father Illuminato brought the news himself, his face solemn.

"It will not be easy," he said. We sat in the convent garden, where spring bulbs had pushed green shoots through the soil. "They have influence, money, and the weight of custom on their side."

"And what do I have?"

"The law," he replied. "And truth."

The law. It seemed a fragile thing to stake everything on, this code I could not read and only partially understood. Yet it was all there was.

"Will you speak for me?" I asked. "Before the magistrate?"

He shook his head. "The Cardinal has engaged Illuminato Checchini, a lawyer of some repute, known for his opposition to slavery. He wishes to meet with you tomorrow to prepare your testimony."

My testimony. The words sent a chill through me. What story could I tell that would hold against theirs? I was not eloquent. I was barely literate. I could not even be certain of my own age.

"Another Illuminato," I said, managing a small smile.

"A good omen, perhaps." He returned it.

Illuminato Checchini arrived the next morning, a slight man with piercing eyes and a beard streaked through with grey. He spoke rapidly, hands in constant motion.

"The case rests on two pillars," he said, pacing the parlor while I sat with my hands folded, working to follow his Italian. "First, that Italian law does not recognize slavery within its borders. Second, that you were brought to Italy from a country where slavery was already illegal under Ottoman law."

He stopped and fixed me with a direct gaze. "I need to know everything. How you were captured, who owned you, how you came to Italy. Leave nothing out, no matter how painful."

For the first time since my arrival in Italy, I told the whole of it. Not in fragments, but a continuous account. The raid on the village. The march across the desert. The succession of masters. The scars carved into my flesh.

The sea crossing. The years of service. He listened without interruption, taking notes, his face betraying nothing but a tightening around the eyes when I described the branding.

"And you wish to remain with the sisters?" he asked when I finished. "Not return to Africa, or seek employment elsewhere?"

"Yes," I said. "I wish to serve God as I have been served here."

He made a final note. "The Michielis will argue that they have treated you well, that you owe them for your keep, that the child needs you. They may suggest the sisters have unduly influenced you."

"No one has influenced me." The steadiness of my own voice surprised me. "I chose this with my own will. A will given to me by God, not by any person in this house."

A small smile crossed his lips. "Hold to exactly that before the magistrate."

The day of the hearing dawned cold and damp, rain falling in a fine mist that beaded on cloaks and gathered in the dips of cobblestones as we made our way through the city. I wore my blue dress and a black shawl borrowed from a novice. The silver cross hung at my throat, visible.

The courthouse was stone and marble, its corridors wide and echoing. I had never entered such a building. The high ceilings and polished floors pressed on me, the weight of authority made visible, the architecture of power I had never been invited to address.

We were led to a small courtroom. A magistrate in black robes sat behind a raised desk. The Michielis were already present, seated with their lawyer, a heavyset man with florid cheeks and a gold watch chain stretched across his waist. Mimmina was not with them. I was grateful for that.

The proceedings opened with formalities I barely followed, names recorded, documents presented, legal phrases exchanged between the lawyers. I sat still, hands clasped in my lap.

The Michielis' lawyer spoke first; his voice trained for rooms like this one.

"Your Honor, my clients have acted with nothing but benevolence toward this woman. They rescued her from a life of certain misery in Africa, brought her to civilization, clothed her, fed her, and treated her as part of their household. In return, they ask only for the fulfillment of her duties, duties she willingly performed until the sisters filled her head with notions above her station."

He described the Michielis' investment, the child's attachment to me, the disruption my absence had caused. He produced the papers with a flourish, presenting them to the magistrate as one presents evidence of the obvious.

"These documents establish my clients' right to this woman's service," he concluded. "We ask the court to enforce this arrangement and return her to her rightful place."

Throughout his speech I kept my eyes lowered, aware of the signora's gaze pressing against the side of my face. I glanced up once and met her eyes.

What lived there was not hatred, but something colder than that. The affronted dignity of one whose property has developed an inconvenient will of its own.

Then Illuminato Checchini rose.

"Your Honor," he began, his voice quieter than his opponent's but no less clear, "this case is not about contracts or investments or even gratitude. It is about a fundamental principle upon which our nation is built, that no human being can be the property of another."

He moved to stand beside me, his hand resting briefly on the back of my chair. "Josephine Margaret Bakhita sits before you today not as an object to be claimed but as a woman asserting her legal right to freedom. She was born free in Sudan, taken by force, and sold against her will. Neither Ottoman law, which governed Sudan at the time of her capture, nor Italian law, which governs us here today, recognizes the legitimacy of these transactions."

He laid out his documents. Legal opinions, precedents, statements from the Cardinal and from those who opposed the trade in persons across Europe. His argument was methodical, each point laid upon the last, a case built not merely for my freedom but for the principle that freedom was my natural state, regardless of what had been done to me.

"The question before this court is simple," he concluded. "Does Josephine Bakhita have the right to determine her own future? Italian law says yes. Human dignity says yes. Justice says yes."

The magistrate, who had listened to both arguments with a face that revealed nothing, turned to me.

"Josephine Bakhita," he said, "you have heard both arguments. What do you wish to say on your own behalf?"

I had not expected to be addressed. I steadied myself, looked first at Checchini, who nodded, then at Mother Superior, whose gaze was level and still.

"Your Honor," I began, my voice quiet but firm, "I am grateful to the Michielis for their kindness to me. They gave me shelter when I had none, food when I was hungry. They did not beat me or starve me, as others had before them."

I paused. "But kindness is not freedom. Care is not dignity. I have found with the sisters not just shelter for my body, but recognition of my soul. I have been baptized into a faith that holds all persons equal before God. I cannot return to a life where I am property, even property that is well-treated."

The magistrate was still for a moment, studying me, the set of his face changing in some way I could not name, a pause before he spoke that had not been there before.

"And if the court rules against you?" he asked. "If you are legally bound to return to the Michielis' service?"

The question reached me where I had not fortified myself. I had not looked past the immediate struggle to what failure would mean.

"Then I will go," I said finally, "because I respect the law. But I will go as Josephine Bakhita, not as a possession. And I will pray that one day, no person will be owned by another, in this country or any other."

A murmur moved through the room. The magistrate raised his hand for quiet, then closed the file before him.

"I will consider the arguments presented today. My ruling will be delivered in three days' time."

Those three days passed like water through cracked stone. I worked in the garden, scrubbed floors, sat with the sisters at prayer. Anything to keep my hands occupied and my mind from the courtroom. The sisters did not press me to speak. They were simply present, and that steadiness was its own kind of grace.

On the third day, we returned. The same room, the same magistrate, the same lawyers. But the air itself had shifted, a tension without a source, only a quality of held breath.

The magistrate entered, took his seat, and addressed the room without preamble.

"Having considered the arguments presented, the relevant laws, and the principles of justice upon which our nation stands, I rule as follows."

He looked at me then, his gaze neither warm nor cold, simply direct.

"Josephine Margaret Bakhita is declared a free woman under Italian law. The documents claiming ownership are invalid within our borders. She is at liberty to choose her own path, whether that be with the Canossian Sisters or elsewhere."

The words entered me slowly, the way warmth enters cold hands, not all at once, but spreading inward from the edges. For a moment I could not move, could not locate the boundary of my own body. The chains that had held me for as long as I could remember, first iron, then invisible, but no less real, had just been named, in a room of polished marble, by a man in black robes, as what they had always been: unlawful.

Free. Legally free.

The Michielis' lawyer protested immediately, his voice rising with talk of appeals and higher courts. The signora's face had gone white. The signor sat perfectly still, his expression unreadable.

None of it reached me.

I was already rising. Turning toward Mother Superior, whose serene face now held a quiet smile.

"Come, Josephine," she said, extending her hand. "Let us go home."

I took it. As we left the courtroom, I did not look back toward the Michielis' table. There was nothing more to say, nothing to defend or explain.

The rain had stopped. Weak sunlight moved across the stones as we came out of the building, and the city opened before us, its canals, bridges, and domes, its centuries of accumulated human life. The same Venice that had received me as property now watched me walk out through its streets as something else entirely.

Father Illuminato fell into step beside us. After a moment, he asked, "What will you do now?"

I touched the cross at my throat, its weight familiar, its edges known to my fingers. Not a burden. Not a chain. A choice made and kept.

I lifted my face to the thin January sun and walked on, and did not answer.

Chapter Twelve

Freedom was not what I had expected. I had imagined it as a gate swinging open, one side captivity, the other liberty, the crossing instantaneous. Instead, it came in small discoveries, each one arriving when I was not looking for it. The morning I walked to the chapel without calculating whether the sound of my footsteps would displease anyone. The afternoon I sat in the garden for ten unaccounted-for minutes, and no one came to find me. The evening I chose to read instead of sleep, and the choice belonged entirely to me.

No longer property. The thought still arrived unbidden, at prayer, in the garden, in the dark before dawn. Each time I noticed my shoulders had not drawn in against it. The body, it seemed, was learning before the mind could catch up.

"What will you do with your freedom?" Mother Superior asked one evening in early May, when tulips had opened along the garden wall and the air carried the scent of rain-washed stone. We sat beneath an ancient olive tree, watching swallows cut the darkening sky.

I had been turning the question over for weeks. In the immediate aftermath of the ruling, I had been occupied simply with the fact of it, the astonishing, still-unfamiliar fact of it. Now the question of shape pressed on me.

"I wish to stay," I said. "If you will have me."

She nodded, unsurprised. "As a postulant? You are considering religious life?"

The question startled me. I had not imagined myself in the black habit of the sisters, bound by vows. Yet something in the word resonated and did not let go.

"Is such a thing possible?" I asked. "For someone like me?"

Her eyes, usually so serene, sharpened briefly. "Someone who has suffered greatly, who has shown remarkable courage, who has chosen faith over security? Yes, Josephine. It is possible."

I lowered my gaze. Even now, after everything, I still carried the habit of seeing myself as less than others.

"I would need to learn so much more," I said.

"Yes," she agreed. "And that learning begins now, whether or not you eventually take vows. There is much we can teach you, and much you can teach us."

The next morning she summoned me to her office, a spare, neat room overlooking the canal. On her desk lay several books, a stack of fresh paper, and a small wooden box inlaid with mother-of-pearl.

"Tools for the journey ahead," she said.

I approached the books first. A primer of Italian grammar, well-worn but carefully maintained.

"I already know some letters," I said, not wanting to seem ungrateful, aware of my limitations.

"Yes. But now you will learn in order, not in fragments. Sister Fabretti will work with you each morning."

She opened the wooden box to reveal pens, ink, and a small knife for sharpening quills. Then she held out a leather-bound journal, its pages blank, the cover the color of dark soil.

"Your reflections," she said. "Your thoughts, prayers, memories, whatever you wish to preserve. The spiritual life requires attention. Writing helps us see more clearly what God is doing within us."

My first lesson with Sister Fabretti began the following day. She was older than most of the sisters, her hands gnarled by arthritis, her eyes the color of faded denim, pale, precise, missing nothing. We sat in a small room near the library, sunlight falling through high windows, and she drew the full alphabet on a slate in a single uninterrupted motion.

"You know some already," she said. It was not a question.

I recited what I had. She listened without expression, then held out the chalk. "Show me."

I took it, its powdery texture familiar against my fingers, and reproduced the letters I knew. My hand shook slightly with the effort of precision. When I finished, she studied the slate for a long moment.

"Your A leans," she said. "Fix it."

I fixed it. She watched. "Again."

We spent the entire first lesson on three letters. Not because I could not learn them, but because she would not move forward until I had mastered them fully. By the end, my hand ached and my A stood straight.

"Tomorrow," she said, setting down the chalk, "four more."

I walked back to my room with the taste of chalk dust on my lips and something lighter in my chest that it took me a moment to name. It was not joy exactly. It was the satisfaction of a thing done correctly. A satisfaction I had never been permitted to feel in a life of labour performed for others.

Day by day, letters became words. Words became sentences. In the evenings I sat at the small desk in my room with the journal Mother Superior had given me. At first the entries were simple:

Today I learned five new words. The garden is blooming. I helped prepare the soup.

But as the weeks passed and my skill grew, something else began to surface.

I remembered something today, I wrote one evening in late May. *The sound of my mother singing as she ground millet for the morning meal. Her voice was low and sweet. I cannot recall the words of her song, but the melody lives in my bones.*

Another night:

The scars on my body are a map of where I have been, not where I am going. Christ's wounds remained after His resurrection, not as reminders of suffering, but as proof of love's victory over death. Perhaps mine, too, can speak of victory rather than defeat.

And later still:

The sisters treat me as one of them. Not a curiosity, not a project, not a servant. A companion. I did not know such a thing was possible. I am still learning it is real.

Summer advanced, bringing a heat that carried traces of Africa in it, though Venice's wet air differed from the dry scorch of Sudan. The convent garden flourished. Roses climbed the stone walls. Herbs grew in neat beds, their scents released by the brush of skirts as the sisters moved among them. Vegetables ripened in orderly rows.

One afternoon in July, Sister Angelica and I were harvesting beans, the pods snapping crisply between our fingers, when she paused in her work and looked at me.

"You have a gift," she said. "The plants respond to you."

I looked up, surprised. "I only do what you have taught me."

She shook her head. "No. You listen to them. Most people speak to plants, if they speak at all. You listen."

I turned a bean pod in my fingers, considering this. "Perhaps," I said slowly, "it is because I know what it is to be treated as less than human. I do not wish to treat anything with such disregard, not even the smallest herb."

She was quiet for a moment. "That," she said, "is wisdom that cost a great deal."

We worked on in silence, the sound of the pods snapping between us, the smell of warm earth rising from the beds.

In October, Sister Fabretti brought me to assist with the children who came for catechism on Wednesday afternoons. Sons and daughters of shopkeepers, artisans, and fishermen, their faces scrubbed, their manner subdued until they passed through the convent gates, and then transformed: curious, energetic, occasionally mischievous.

They regarded me with wide eyes. Most had never seen someone with skin as dark as mine. They whispered, pointed when they thought I was not watching, directed their questions to Sister Fabretti with sidelong glances at me.

Is she from Africa? Why is her skin so dark? Does she speak Italian?

Sister Fabretti answered each question with patience and firmness. Over the following weeks their wonder gave way to something easier. I became simply the one who told the best stories, who could identify birds by their songs, who never seemed to mind when lessons ran long.

One boy in particular, small, copper-haired, perpetually scraped at the knee, sought me out before every lesson. He would appear at my elbow and place something in my palm: a smooth stone, a bent nail, a feather found on his way to the convent.

"For you, Sister," he would say, very solemn.

I kept them all on the windowsill in my room, where the morning light found them first.

In November, I fell ill.

It began as a scratchy throat and a heaviness in the chest, the kind of thing one works through and forgets. Within two days it had become a fever that burned day and night, leaving me weak and confused. The sisters moved me to the infirmary, a quiet room near the chapel, and Sister Margherita applied poultices and spooned broth and sat with me through the worst hours.

In the delirium, past and present collapsed into each other. I called out in the language of my childhood. Reached for hands long gone. Shrank from blows that existed only in memory.

"She is traveling far," Sister Margherita said quietly to someone near the door. "We must pray her back to us."

Nine days. Then the fever broke, leaving me soaked and clear-eyed and exhausted in the way of someone returned from a long distance. I opened my eyes to find Mother Superior seated beside my bed, her rosary moving slowly through her fingers.

"Welcome back," she said.

My throat was too raw for speech. She brought water, supporting my head while I drank.

"God has more work for you here," she said simply.

Through the infirmary window I could see the convent garden, stripped bare by November winds. The trees stood against the grey sky, their branches precise and dark as ink marks. The herb beds lay dormant. Even the roses had been cut back, their canes stubbed low against the earth.

When I was strong enough to hold a pen, I wrote: *I am like that garden. Stripped back, dormant, but not dead. What will grow from this soil in the season to come?*

By Christmas I had regained my strength. I helped the sisters arrange the crèche, the Holy Family, the shepherds, the Magi, and last of all the tiny carved figure of the Christ child, laid reverently in the straw.

After Midnight Mass, when the others had retired, I knelt alone before the crèche in the candlelight. The chapel was very still. Wax dripped. The eternal flame before the tabernacle barely moved.

God had come into the world not as a king or a warrior, but as a child who could be carried, who depended on human hands for everything.

"You came to serve," I whispered to the small wooden figure. "Teach me to do the same."

The new year, 1893, arrived cold and bright. My lessons with Sister Fabretti advanced to more complex texts: the letters of St Paul, the writings of St Augustine, passages from the Gospels.

One morning she watched me work through a passage from John without assistance and said simply, "Your pronunciation has improved greatly."

"I practice," I said. I did not mention the hours spent reading aloud to myself by candlelight after the convent was asleep.

She nodded, marking our place in the text with one gnarled finger. "Understanding is good. But some mysteries cannot be understood at all. They can only be lived."

I thought of that long afterward.

In February, Mother Superior called me to her office. The room was empty of gifts this time. She sat behind her desk, hands folded.

"Josephine," she said, "it has been nearly a year since the court declared you free. In that time, you have made remarkable progress in your studies and in your spiritual formation."

I waited.

"The time has come for a decision. If you wish to formally enter religious life as a postulant, the community is prepared to receive you. If you wish to remain as a lay associate, or to seek a different path entirely, we support that choice equally."

The moment settled over me. I had known this was coming, had felt it approaching for weeks. Now it arrived and I held it, not with fear, but with a kind of stillness.

"I need time to pray," I said.

"Take the time you need."

For three days I moved through the convent as though seeing it for the first time. I watched the sisters at prayer, at work, at rest. I spent long hours in the chapel before the crucifix. I walked in the winter garden, where green shoots had begun to push through the cold earth, thin and pale and insistent.

On the third evening I opened my journal.

> *I have been asked to choose. But perhaps the choice was made long ago, when I first looked at the man on the cross and recognized in His wounds a reflection of my own. Perhaps I have been walking this path since the moment I learned there was a God who knew what it meant to suffer, to be abandoned, to die, and yet to rise again.*

I came to this place as property. I remain as a person, free to go or stay as I choose. And I choose to stay, not from fear, not from habit, not from lack of options, but from love. Love for this community that has become my family. Love for the God who has led me through desert and sea to this place. Love for the work of bringing light into darkness, wherever it may be found.

Tomorrow I will tell Mother Superior: yes.

The next morning, after Mass, I found her in the garden inspecting the rose canes for frost damage, her breath clouding in the cold air.

"I have decided," I said.

She waited, her hands still on the canes, allowing the choice to be entirely mine.

"I wish to enter religious life," I said. "To become a Canossian Sister, if you will have me."

Her face stayed composed, but her eyes warmed. "Are you certain this is your vocation, Josephine? That God is calling you, not merely that we have need of you, or that this life has been kind to you?"

"Yes," I said, and the word carried everything behind it. "I have been lost and found, enslaved and freed. Now I choose to bind myself to something greater than my own will. Not from fear. From love."

She nodded once. Then she reached out and took my hand, her pale fingers against my dark ones, both of them rough from garden work, both marked by what life had made of them.

"Then we welcome you, Josephine Margaret Bakhita, as a postulant of the Canossian Daughters of Charity. May God who has begun this good work in you bring it to completion."

Somewhere above us a bird called once, and then it was quiet.

Chapter Thirteen

The day of my clothing ceremony dawned white with frost. December 1896. Three years since I had entered as a postulant, learning the rhythms and requirements of religious life. Three years of study, prayer, and service. Three years of becoming something new while carrying all that I had been.

Now the final threshold waited.

I knelt in the chapel before dawn, alone with the flickering sanctuary lamp and the first pale light seeping through the stained glass. My postulant's dress, the simple blue I had worn these three years, felt suddenly significant in the way of garments about to be shed forever. I ran my fingers over the worn fabric, remembering the woman who had first put it on. So tentative. So wounded. So desperate to belong.

"Are you ready?" Mother Superior's voice came softly from behind me.

I rose from my knees. "Yes. And no. Both at once."

She smiled, the expression softening the austere planes of her face. "As it should be. No bride comes to her wedding without trembling."

The phrase no longer startled me as it once had. I had learned its meaning through the long novitiate, not a denial of my womanhood, but its consecration. Not an escape from love, but love's fulfillment in ways I was still discovering.

The ceremony was set for ten o'clock. As the hour approached, sisters and novices moved through the convent with quiet purpose, arranging flowers in the chapel, preparing the meal that would follow, laying out the habit I would soon wear. Black wool, stark and unadorned.

I was led to a small anteroom where Sister Fabretti waited with scissors and a silver basin of water.

"Kneel," she said gently.

The cool stone floor pressed through the thin fabric of my dress. She moved behind me, her hands steady despite her years.

"In the early Church," she said, gathering my hair in her fingers, "women cut their hair when they took religious vows. A sign of renunciation. Of leaving behind worldly beauty for God alone."

The scissors made a soft, decisive sound near my ear. The weight of my hair fell away, coil by coil, until nothing remained but the shortest layer against my scalp. Each snip severed something. Not erasing my former life, but changing what it meant.

When she had finished, Sister Fabretti held a mirror before me. The face that looked back was both familiar and strange, my features made more prominent by the absence of hair, my eyes larger, my expression more exposed. I looked younger and older at once, more vulnerable, yet somehow stronger.

"Now," she said, setting aside the mirror. "We wash."

The water in the basin had been blessed by the bishop who would preside over the ceremony. As Sister Fabretti poured it over my shorn head, murmuring prayers in Latin, a memory arrived without warning, another washing, years ago, when I had been baptized. Then, too, water had marked a crossing, a cleansing, a new beginning.

This washing felt different. Not the dramatic rebirth of baptism, but something gentler, the way rainwater slowly reshapes stone. I had been Josephine Margaret Bakhita for years. Today I would become Sister Josephine, taking my place fully among the Daughters of Charity.

When the washing was complete, I was dressed in the habit for the first time, the black woolen dress falling in severe lines to my ankles, the white collar crisp at my throat, the rosary beads at my waist. The fabric was heavier than I had expected.

"The veil is the last piece," said Sister Fabretti, holding up the black cloth. "It is not placed until the ceremony itself."

I touched my bare scalp with tentative fingers. The absence of hair felt like an opening, a space cleared for whatever was to come.

The chapel was full when I entered. Sisters from our convent and others nearby. Priests who had been part of my instruction. A few trusted friends. Candles blazed on the altar, their light catching the gold thread of the bishop's vestments as he stood waiting, pastoral staff in hand.

I walked the center aisle alone, my steps measured, my eyes on the crucifix above the altar. Christ's face looked down. Not with pity, not with judgment, but with a recognition that still startled me with its intimacy. He knew what it was to bear scars. He knew what it was to be stripped, exposed, remade.

I lay prostrate before the altar, arms outstretched in the shape of the cross, while the Litany of Saints was chanted above me. The stone floor pressed cold and hard against my body. I did not resist the discomfort. It was another reminder of what I was undertaking.

I rose when bidden, knelt before the bishop, and spoke.

"I, Josephine Margaret Bakhita, vow to almighty God poverty, chastity, and obedience according to the rule of the Canossian Daughters of Charity, so help me God and His holy Gospel."

My voice neither shook nor faltered. Whatever doubts had troubled me in the silent watches of the night, whatever fears had whispered of unworthiness or incapacity, all were silenced in this moment. I had chosen. And in choosing, found a freedom deeper than the mere absence of constraint.

The bishop placed the veil upon my head, arranging it with careful hands until it framed my face and fell in soft folds to my shoulders.

"Receive this veil," he intoned, "as a sign of your consecration to Christ, the heavenly Bridegroom."

The final blessing was given. Prayers were said. Newly veiled and vowed, I turned to face the congregation for the first time as Sister Josephine Bakhita.

The faces that looked back were solemn, some wet with tears, others bright with joy. But one face stopped me. A young novice from Milan, arrived only weeks before, stared not at my veil or habit, but at my hands, where the scars from the old branding remained visible, raised patterns against my dark skin.

I met her gaze steadily. I neither hid my hands nor drew attention to them. Both were part of me, the veil and the scars, and both would remain.

At the modest celebration that followed, the young novice approached me hesitantly.

"Forgive me, Sister," she said, her voice barely above a whisper. "I did not mean to stare. Your hands, what happened to them?"

I looked down at them, strong from years of garden work, marked by my earliest memories of slavery.

"I was a slave," I said. "In Sudan, and later in other parts of Africa. These are the marks of my masters."

Her eyes widened. "A slave? But how, how did you come to be here?"

Around us the celebration continued, sisters talking, sharing bread and wine, beginning to clear the remains of the meal.

"It is a long story," I said. "Perhaps another time."

She nodded, clearly disappointed but too well-formed in her training to press further. As she turned to go, I heard my own voice behind her.

"Come to the garden tomorrow, after vespers. I will tell you then."

That night, alone in my cell, I removed my veil and habit with reverent care, folding each piece according to custom before putting on the simple linen nightdress.

By the light of a single candle, the raised patterns across my abdomen and chest where I had been cut with knives. The round, puckered mark on my right shoulder from the branding iron. The fine white lines across my back from whippings whose occasions I could no longer recall individually.

I touched each mark. Not with shame, but with acknowledgment. These were the stations of a road I had walked without knowing its name or destination.

The young novice's question had opened something in me. Behind it waited not just my story, but the stories of countless others who had walked the same road, many without finding the freedom I now held.

The next day passed in the convent's accustomed rhythm, prayer, work, meals in silence broken only by scripture reading. I moved through each hour with outward composure while inwardly rehearsing and discarding different ways to begin a story I had never fully told, not even to myself.

After vespers I went to the garden. The novice was already there, seated on the stone bench beneath the olive tree, hands folded, her face turning toward me as I approached, eager, apprehensive, innocent in ways I had never been.

"Sister Josephine," she said, rising. "I wasn't sure you would come."

"I promised," I said simply, gesturing for her to sit. I settled beside her, still adjusting to the unfamiliar weight of the habit.

The garden held the last light of the day. The air carried rosemary and the metallic edge that precedes frost. A blackbird sang from the convent wall, its melody brief and liquid, then gone.

"My name was not always Josephine," I began. "I was born in a village in Sudan around 1869. I do not know the exact year. My family gave me another name; one I no longer remember."

For a moment, the words sat in my mouth without moving. I pressed my palms flat against my knees, feeling the rough wool of the habit, and then the first sentence found its way out, and the next followed, and the next.

I told her of the fragments I still carried from my childhood. The village. The fields. The rhythms of a world now accessible to me only in dreams.

Then came the harder part. The raid. The kidnapping. The first sale. The succession of masters. The branding. The beatings. The daily erosion of a life without dignity.

As I spoke, the novice's face moved through shock, then horror, then a profound and wordless compassion that brought tears to her eyes. She did not look away, even when my narrative touched on things no sheltered European girl should have needed to imagine.

"The Turkish officer's wife," I said, "would beat us for pleasure, not punishment. She used a cane on the soles of our feet, where the pain is most acute and the marks least visible."

The novice's clasped hands tightened until her knuckles showed pale through the skin. Still, she listened.

I spoke of the journey to Italy with Legnani. The Michielis. The first encounter with the crucifix at the Catechumenate. The court case. The baptism. The slow discovery of vocation.

"And now," I said, as twilight deepened and the first stars appeared above the eastern wall, "I am here. Sister Josephine Bakhita, Canossian Daughter of Charity."

She was weeping openly, tears moving unchecked down her pale cheeks. "How can you speak of it so calmly?" she asked. "How can you bear the memory?"

The question deserved a truthful answer.

"I bear it because I must," I said. "The memories are part of me, as surely as these scars." I held my hands out, palms up. "But they no longer have the power to define me. They are what happened to me. Not who I am."

She studied my hands, then my face.

"And you forgive them?" she asked. "The ones who did this?"

"I try," I said. "Some days better than others. It is a journey, not a destination."

We sat in silence as darkness came fully down. The garden disappeared into shadow around us.

The convent bell rang. We rose together, straightening our habits.

"Thank you," she said. "For trusting me with your story."

I nodded, and did not say what I was already beginning to understand, that the telling had given back something I had not known was missing.

I mentioned this to Father Illuminato at our next spiritual direction session.

"It is no surprise," he said, his face thoughtful in the dim light of his study. "The Word became flesh, Scripture tells us. There is power in giving flesh to our experiences through words, in making the invisible visible, the unspeakable spoken."

I turned the thought over slowly. "So, my story might have value beyond myself? It might serve some purpose?"

"All stories have purpose," he replied. "Especially those that bear witness to both the depths of human cruelty and the heights of divine mercy."

A month after my profession, Mother Superior called me to her office. Winter had settled fully over Venice, the garden under a thin blanket of snow, the canals freezing at their edges, the convent busy with preparations for Christmas.

"I have received a request," she said, her voice measured. "From the pastor at San Trovaso. He is organizing a mission week in January and wishes you to speak to the congregation about your experiences."

I stared at her. "My experiences?"

"Your journey from slavery to religious life. He believes your testimony would be powerful, given the Church's increasing work against the slave trade."

To speak publicly, to strangers, about things so personal, so raw. The prospect filled me with a dread I could not immediately name. It was not simply the fear of an audience. It was the fear of making my wounds the object of strangers' examination.

"I am not eloquent," I said. "And my Italian, though improved, is still imperfect."

"It is not eloquence he seeks. As for your Italian, it is more than adequate."

"You are not ordered to accept," she added, reading my silence correctly. "It is a request. Pray about it. Consider what good might come from such witness."

In the days that followed I knelt before the tabernacle, wrote pages in my journal, spoke with Father Illuminato and Sister Fabretti. Gradually, reluctantly, a clarity came. Not eagerness, but something quieter than that. An understanding that perhaps my scars were meant not only for my own redemption, but for others' awakening. That in speaking of slavery's reality, I might contribute in some small way to its end.

I sent word to Mother Superior: yes.

The day arrived cold and bright, the sky a sharp blue above Venice's rooftops. I traveled to San Trovaso with Sister Angelica, both of us wrapped in extra wool against the January cold. The church was larger than our convent chapel, its space filled with the mingled scents of incense, candle wax, and the damp wool of winter coats.

The pastor greeted us warmly and showed us to a small room to wait. My prepared notes trembled in my hands. The words I had written seemed suddenly thin, pale against the weight of what they were meant to carry.

"Remember," Sister Angelica said, "you speak not for yourself, but for those who cannot speak. For those still held in chains."

Her words reached something in me and steadied it.

When the time came, I walked to the front of the church with measured steps. The congregation took me in, the black habit and veil, the dark skin, the scars visible on my hands. A stillness fell over the pews, the kind that precedes something not yet understood.

I adjusted my notes and looked out. Rows of faces, all turned toward me. An old woman in the second pew held her rosary in both hands. A man near the back had removed his hat and was turning it slowly by the brim. A young mother held her child against her shoulder and did not look away.

"My name is Sister Josephine Bakhita," I began, my voice soft but clear in the hushed church. "I was born in Sudan around 1869, though I do not know the exact year. When I was perhaps nine years old, I was taken from my village by slave traders."

The story moved through me as it had in the garden with the novice, but differently, less raw, more ordered, as though the first telling had laid out a path I could now follow without losing my footing. I spoke of the succession of masters, physical abuses, the wounds deeper than any visible scar. I described the journey to Italy, the awakening of faith, the legal battle, the discovery of vocation.

At one point, describing the branding, the old constriction rose in my chest, the body's memory of what the mind had learned to contain. I paused.

The old woman in the second pew met my eyes and held them. I drew breath and continued.

"I stand before you today," I said finally, "not as a victim seeking pity, but as a witness to both human cruelty and divine mercy. The same God who met me in my darkest hour waits to meet each of you in yours. The same Christ who bore scars has not removed mine, but has changed what they mean."

The silence that followed was absolute. The silence of people holding something too large to immediately set down. Then, gradually, a collective exhalation moved through the pews. The pastor stepped forward.

"Let us pray," he said, "for all those still held in bondage. And let us give thanks for the witness of Sister Josephine, whose life shows us the transforming power of God's love."

Afterward, several parishioners approached. Some to express gratitude, others to ask questions, a few simply to touch my hand as though something might pass between us. Their responses moved and discomfited me in equal measure. I received each person as I could, and was glad when Sister Angelica gently drew me toward the door.

"You moved them deeply," she observed as we made our way back through the narrowing January light. "Your words found their mark."

I nodded. The telling had cost me more than I had anticipated. Not only the energy of public speech, but the particular exhaustion of having opened old ground before strangers.

Yet something had also shifted. I could not precisely name it. I only knew that as we walked, the city settling into evening around us, the scars on my hands caught the last of the light in the same way they always had. And yet I held them differently.

That night, in the quiet of my cell, I stood before the small mirror used for adjusting the veil. Sister Josephine Bakhita looked back at me, black habit, shorn head beneath the veil, dark skin, scarred hands. I raised one hand and pressed my fingertips to the glass, as I had done on the morning of my baptism, as I had done on the morning I first stood in Sorella Maria's small room and did not recognise the woman in the white dress. The glass held the impression for a moment, then cleared.

Chapter Fourteen

Spring came early to Venice in 1897. By late February, crocuses had pushed through the convent garden's thawing soil, their purple and gold blossoms sharp and clean against the last grey of winter. The air softened, carrying hints of salt from the lagoon and the first tentative perfume of awakening earth. Even the stone walls seemed to exhale, releasing the damp chill that had clung to them through the darkest months.

Three months since I had taken my vows.

Three months of wearing the habit, of answering to Sister Josephine, of living into promises that bound me more profoundly than any chains ever had. Three months during which my testimony at San Trovaso had led to other invitations, other parishes, other congregations, other listeners who came wanting to hear the story of a slave who had become a bride of Christ.

Each telling was both ordeal and release. Each time I spoke of the branding house, of the Turkish officer's cellar, of the march across the desert, those moments returned in the body—the iron's heat, the cane's sting, the thirst that had turned my tongue to leather. Yet each telling also set something further away, transforming the rawness into something not healed, precisely, but purposeful.

"You have become quite the missionary," observed Sister Fabretti one evening, she with her mending, I with a letter I was composing to a parish in Verona that had requested my testimony. "Who would have thought that your suffering would become your apostolate?"

I looked up from the paper, considering her words.

Apostolate. From the Greek for one who is sent. I had been sent, certainly, passed from hand to hand across a continent, transported across a sea, delivered finally to this place. But sent by whom? For what? The questions lingered like incense after vespers, persistent and unanswered.

"I do not think of it as an apostolate," I said. "More as a duty. To speak for those who cannot speak for themselves."

She nodded, her needle flashing in the lamplight. "The voiceless. Yes. There are so many."

The voiceless. The thought stayed with me as I completed my letter, joined the community for evening prayer, retired for the night. How many remained in bondage even now, as I moved freely through a life I had chosen? How many bore scars like mine, without the balm of faith or community?

I knew what the missionary journals reported. Millions still enslaved across Africa, in the Ottoman Empire, in parts of Asia. Women and children sold for a handful of coins. Men worked to death in mines and fields. Families broken apart and scattered.

Against such immensity, what was one voice?

I slept fitfully that night. Dark eyes behind wooden slats. Hands reaching toward something forever out of reach. Mouths open without sound.

In the chapel for morning prayer, the familiar psalms would not settle. The other sisters had filed out, leaving me alone before the tabernacle.

"Sister Josephine." Mother Superior's voice came from the doorway. "You seem troubled."

I rose, smoothing my habit. "I have been thinking about those still enslaved. Those whose stories will never be heard."

She crossed to the pew beside mine and sat. For a moment she said nothing, her eyes on the crucifix.

"To speak for them," she said finally. "This is why you continue to accept these invitations, despite the cost."

"Yes. Though I sometimes wonder if words make any difference. Whether they can truly convey what slavery is."

She was quiet again, the quality of her silence different from ordinary silence. The silence of a woman weighing what is true against what is easy.

"The Cardinal has extended another invitation," she said. "A gathering at the seminary in Padua next month. He is training missionaries who will go to Africa. He believes your story would be valuable for them to hear before they leave."

I nodded my acceptance without hesitation.

That afternoon in the garden, Sister Angelica and I prepared the soil for spring planting. The physical labour was a relief after the morning's turmoil, the rhythm of digging, turning, breaking clumps of earth between my fingers anchoring me in the present moment, in the simple work of preparing ground for seed.

"You're quiet today," she observed, wiping her brow despite the cool air. "More so than usual."

"I have been thinking about freedom," I said, crumbling a handful of dark soil and watching it fall back to the prepared bed. "What it means to have it. What it means to lack it."

She resumed her work with the measured movements of one who had tended gardens for decades. "Freedom is a curious thing. It exists, or doesn't, on so many levels."

"Yes," I said, thinking of the layers of bondage I had known, physical chains, the submission that outlasts the chains, the long interior captivity of believing oneself worthy only of servitude. "Its absence marks not just the body but the soul."

"Yet the soul can be free even when the body is not," she countered, her voice gentle but direct. "The martyrs proved this. So did Christ himself."

I turned this over as we worked. There was truth in it. A deep truth I had glimpsed in my own darkest moments, when something within me had remained inviolate despite everything done to the body that housed it. But it was also true that physical bondage created conditions that starved the soul's flourishing. That the body's freedom and the spirit's were meant to exist together, not in opposition.

"Both matter," I said. "The body's freedom and the soul's. To speak of one without the other risks diminishing the horror of what slavery actually is."

Sister Angelica straightened, her aged face solemn in the afternoon light. "You are right. Forgive me if I seemed to suggest otherwise."

"No forgiveness needed. It has no simple answer."

We completed our work in companionable silence, each following her own thoughts as the garden took shape under our hands, beds marked with string, soil turned and ready, seeds waiting in their packets for tomorrow. When we finished, Sister Angelica blessed the beds with a brief prayer, then patted my arm with soil-stained fingers.

"Your words matter, Josephine," she said. "Never doubt it. They are seeds planted in hearts that might otherwise remain fallow."

That evening, alone at my desk with the journal open, I wrote by the light of the single candle.

Freedom is not only the absence of chains. I think it is also the ability to choose, to say yes or no from one's own conscience. To know that tomorrow is mine to decide.

I have this now. I move through the world not as property but as a person. I speak and am heard. I choose and my choices have weight.

But millions do not have this. They live and die in bondage, their possibilities decided by others' will, their personhood denied, their voices silenced. They are my brothers and sisters.

What do I owe them, I who have crossed from darkness into light? At the very least, to remember. To witness. To speak truth to those willing to hear it. To ensure that the door through which I passed remains open for others to follow.

I paused, the pen hovering above the page.

The door. Throughout my captivity, doors had been symbols of confinement, locked against escape, opened only to admit new suffering. Yet the door of the Catechumenate had opened to receive me as a person, not property. The courthouse door had opened to declare me legally free. The convent door had opened to welcome me as sister, as belonging.

The door remains open, I wrote. *Not just for me. God grant me strength to hold it so, for as long as I have breath and voice.*

The journey to Padua the following month took us through the Venetian countryside at the height of spring. Orchards bloomed in ordered rows. Fields of young wheat moved in the breeze, their green so dense it seemed almost liquid. The air carried the scent of soil and growing things rather than Venice's usual salt.

I traveled with Sister Margherita, whose calm efficiency made her an ideal companion. She handled the train tickets, the lodging at the Paduan convent, the communications with seminary officials, leaving me free to prepare inwardly for what would be the most demanding testimony yet.

The seminary was an imposing structure of pale stone and red tile; its courtyard centered on a fountain where water poured from a lion's mouth into a mosaic-rimmed basin. Young men in black cassocks moved along colonnaded walkways, their voices a low murmur under the splash of water and the cooing of doves in the eaves.

The Cardinal received us in a book-lined study, its walls hung with maps of Africa marked with pins and flags, mission stations, tribal territories, political boundaries. He was older than when I had last seen him at my profession, his once-auburn hair more silver than red, but his eyes were as keen as ever.

“Sister Josephine,” he greeted me, rising from behind his desk. “Thank you for coming. These young men are preparing to go where you have been. Your words may be the difference between approaching those they serve with true respect, or repeating the very patterns of control and possession that created the suffering you have known.”

The weight of this settled over me, not crushing, but substantial with purpose.

“I will speak truth as I know it,” I said.

He nodded. “That is all I ask. And perhaps particular attention to the wounds that require healing beyond the physical, what slavery does within a person, not only to the body.”

The seminary chapel was filled to capacity that evening with seminarians, faculty, religious from nearby communities, and laypeople who had sought permission to attend. The air was heavy with beeswax, incense from the evening's benediction, and the smell of books and close study that permeates places of learning.

At the lectern, I arranged my notes. Rows of faces looked up, young, mostly, their expressions ranging from curiosity to something harder to name. A hunger, perhaps, for an understanding of realities entirely beyond their experience.

"I was born free," I began, departing from my usual opening. "This is the first truth you must understand. No one is born a slave. Slavery is not a natural condition, but a violence against the divine image present in every human being."

A collective intake of breath. A shifting of posture, a sharpening of attention across the pews. This was not the narrative they had perhaps expected, the meek and grateful account of a simple woman saved by European benevolence. This was a claim of inherent dignity. Rights violated rather than benevolence bestowed.

I continued through the familiar arc. The kidnapping, the succession of masters, the abuses, the journey to Italy, the awakening of faith, the legal battle, the discovery of vocation. But differently this time, with particular attention to what had been taken rather than only what had been done. My name. My family. My voice. My agency. The slowly destroyed certainty that I deserved to exist.

"When you go to Africa," I said, looking out at the young men who would soon carry the Gospel to my people, "you will meet many who have known slavery directly or through their parents and grandparents. You will see the wounds, not only on bodies but on souls. Wounds of shame, of rage, of despair, of a trust in human goodness so broken it seems beyond repair."

I paused.

"These wounds cannot be healed by words alone, however well-intentioned. They cannot be answered with theological arguments about suffering's meaning or the universality of sin. They require witness. Presence. A willingness to stand alongside, to listen before speaking, to learn before presuming to teach."

At one point, describing the branding, the old constriction rose in my chest. A young seminarian in the third row, dark-haired, slight, his face still carrying the softness of recent boyhood, met my eyes without looking away. I drew breath and continued.

"I am one voice," I said, my tone quieter. "One story among millions. I stand before you not because my suffering was unique or my redemption more complete, but because circumstances brought me to a place where my voice could be heard. For each one like me who escapes and finds freedom, countless others remain captive, not only in physical chains but in every system that denies full humanity, that extracts labor without honoring the person who performs it."

I looked down at my hands, the scars visible even in the chapel's dim light.

"When you go, remember this: you go not as those who possess something others lack, but as fellow servants of the same God. The Gospel you bring belongs as fully to those you serve as it does to you. And its message of liberation, of dignity, of each person known and beloved by God, must live in every choice you make, every manner in which you approach those you have come to serve."

I closed on the Cardinal's question about interior wounds. The shame that burrows bone-deep, the long difficulty of trusting again after trust has been systematically destroyed.

"This healing is the work of years," I concluded. "It begins with recognition, seeing the full humanity of another person, honoring their story, standing with them in their pain without attempting to diminish or explain it. This is what Christ did. This is what you are called to do."

The chapel was utterly still. Then, slowly, the Cardinal rose, and the entire assembly rose with him. No applause. It would have been wrong in that space. But they stood, and the standing said what applause could not.

That night, in the small guest room at the Paduan convent, sleep would not come. The testimony had taken more from me than usual. Not only the energy of sustained public speech, but the particular cost of pressing into territory I had not reached in previous tellings.

I sat at the window. The garden below lay silvered by moonlight, ordinary shrubs made sculptural in the dark. Beyond the convent walls, the city was quiet with the occasional footstep, the distant bark of a dog, the bells marking the hour from a tower I could not see.

How unlikely this life. A woman born in a Sudanese village, sold in a Khartoum market, transported across the Mediterranean, now seated at a window in Padua, her words received with the respect given to those whose testimony carries weight. The path from there to here was not luck. Something had been present even in the darkest hours, working toward a purpose that could not then have been imagined.

Sleep came finally, reluctantly.

And then the dream.

The slave market at Khartoum. The familiar nightmare landscape. The heat, the dust, the stench of unwashed bodies and barely contained terror.

Around me stood other captives, women, men, children, their eyes vacant or burning with a rage that had nowhere to go. Before them paced the buyers, discussing prices with the unhurried certainty of men conducting ordinary commerce.

But this time, something was different.

I was not bound. I wore my habit, the black wool stark against the market's dust, the white wimple framing my face.

And there, standing at the market's edge, where I had never seen anything before but more barred walls and packed earth, a door. Simple wood, standing open to a landscape of green beyond. Not the gate through which new captives were brought in. Not the exit through which the purchased were led away. A door I had never seen in any previous version of this dream.

A woman near me noticed it. She held a child against her chest, and her eyes moved from the buyers to the open door, and something shifted in them. Not yet hope, but the faint precondition of it. The recognition that there was something to look toward.

Then an old man raised his head. A youth whose eyes had been fixed on the ground.

I took a step toward the door. Then another.

I woke with tears on my face, cool and slow, nothing like the tears of the nightmare, which came fast and hot and wrenched from somewhere deep. I lay still for a moment, listening to Sister Margherita's quiet breathing, watching the dark ceiling.

Outside the window, the sky at the horizon had deepened to the blue that precedes first light. The stars still bright, but already beginning their retreat.

I rose and dressed in the dark, and went to the chapel alone for morning prayer. The familiar words of the psalms moved through me, entering, filling.

The door remains open.

Not a thought I formed. A thing I knew, settled somewhere below thought, the way the body knows warmth.

I knelt and let the morning come.

That phrase stayed with me as we journeyed back to Venice later that day. As I resumed my duties at the convent. As I continued in the months and years ahead to accept invitations to speak wherever I was called.

I had not freed myself. I had been freed. By the courage of those who spoke for me, by the law that named my humanity when custom denied it, by the God who had known me before I could name Him and called me by a name that was mine alone.

But having been freed, something was asked of me in return.

I would stand near the door. I would make it visible. I would call toward those still in the market, not with the voice of someone who had escaped and left them behind, but with the voice of someone who had walked the same ground, borne the same marks, and found that the door had been open all along.

Chapter Fifteen

The summons came in early autumn of 1902, when the convent garden in Venice was heavy with ripening fruit and the first fallen leaves skittered across the flagstones in the morning wind. I had been a professed sister for nearly six years. Years of deepening faith, of continued testimony, of finding my place within the rhythms of religious life.

Mother Superior called me to her office after morning Mass. The room remained as I had always known it, spare, functional, the wooden crucifix on the wall behind her desk. She sat with hands folded, her face composed, yet holding something I could not immediately read.

"Sister Josephine," she began. "I have received a letter from the Provincial Superior."

I nodded, waiting. The Provincial oversaw all Canossian houses in northern Italy. Her word carried the weight of authority second only to Rome itself.

"You are being assigned to our house in Schio. They have need of an experienced sister to assist with the school and infirmary."

Schio. Vaguely familiar. A town somewhere inland, at the foot of mountains whose names I did not know. Not a major city, not a place of particular significance in anything I had ever read or heard.

"When?" I asked.

"In three weeks' time. This will allow for proper transition of your duties here."

Three weeks. I had been in Venice for nearly fourteen years, first at the Catechumenate, then as postulant, novice, professed sister. These walls, these gardens, these canals were the landscape of my freedom, my becoming. A small, cold space opened in my chest at the thought of leaving them.

"May I ask why I have been chosen?" The question slipped out before I could weigh its propriety. It was not our custom to question assignments. Obedience was among the vows I had taken willingly, understanding its cost.

Mother Superior did not seem offended. "Several reasons. Your experience with young children, your skill in the infirmary, your particular testimony." She paused. "And perhaps it is time for you to be known for more than your past, Sister Josephine. In Venice, you will always be primarily the former slave who became a nun. In Schio, you can simply be a Daughter of Charity, serving God's children."

The words struck with unexpected force. Despite my profession and years of service, in Venice I remained defined largely by my history, the miraculous tale used to inspire the faithful and challenge the comfortable. To many I was still more symbol than sister, more story than person.

"I understand," I said, bowing my head slightly. "I will prepare for departure."

"The community will miss you," she added, her voice softening. "As will I. But we do not join religious life to remain comfortable or unchallenged. We go where we are needed, where God can best use us."

The news spread quickly through the convent. The sisters received it with varying degrees of distress and resignation. Some openly tearful, others offering practical advice about what I might expect in Schio. Sister Fabretti, now bent with age but still sharp of mind, sought me out in the garden.

"So, they are sending you away from us," she said, lowering herself carefully onto the stone bench beside me. The autumn sun caught in her spectacles, turning them briefly to discs of light.

"To Schio," I confirmed. "In three weeks."

She nodded, her arthritic hands resting on the head of her walking stick. "A good house. Smaller than this one. The air is cleaner, away from the lagoon. The mountains are visible on clear days."

"The work?" I asked.

"A school for local children, mostly from poor families. A small infirmary. Nothing you have not done here, though with fewer resources and fewer hands."

We sat in silence, watching a pair of sparrows quarrel over crumbs near the kitchen door.

"You fear this change," said Sister Fabretti finally. "After all you have endured, this small upheaval disturbs you deeply."

"Venice has been my home," I said. "The only place where I have known freedom."

She turned to look at me directly, her aged face solemn in the autumn light. "Freedom is not a place, Josephine. It is a condition of the soul. You will carry it with you to Schio, as you have carried it through far darker passages than this."

The three weeks passed with unsettling speed. There were duties to transfer, belongings to pack, farewells to make to the community and the city that had witnessed my transformation.

On the last afternoon I walked to the courthouse alone. I stood outside it for a while, watching the ordinary traffic of a Venetian afternoon pass across the stones where I had once walked out as a legally free woman for the first time. A pair of clerks hurried past with bundled papers. A child led a dog on a rope. The building looked exactly as it always had, stone, marble, indifferent to its own significance.

That was enough. I turned and walked back to the convent through the narrow streets, carrying what needed to be carried.

The morning of departure arrived cold and clear, the canals still and dark in the early light. I attended Mass with the community, received their blessing, embraced those who had been spiritual mothers and sisters to me through all of it. Sister Angelica pressed a small packet of seeds into my hand. Sister Fabretti gave me a book of poetry; its pages marked with pressed flowers from the convent grounds. Mother Superior presented me with a new rosary, its dark wooden beads smooth against my fingers.

The journey to Schio took most of the day, first by boat through the lagoon, then by train across the Veneto plain. As we traveled inland, the landscape shifted. The flat expanses gave way to gentle hills, then steeper rises as we approached the Pre-Alps. The air changed too, becoming sharper, without the perpetual dampness of Venice. I pressed my palm flat against the train window and felt the cold come through the glass, a different cold from what I knew, drier, carrying the faint mineral scent of altitude.

Schio appeared suddenly around a bend. A small town of rust-colored roofs and pale walls in a valley, mountains rising behind it. Church bells rang as our train arrived, marking the hour with bronze voices that echoed across the valley floor.

The convent stood on the town's eastern edge, modest gray stone with a red-tiled roof. It lacked the grandeur of the Venetian house with its centuries of accumulated history. But it had a directness to it, unadorned, uncomplicated, honest in its plainness. Two cypress trees flanked the entrance gate, their dark shapes standing clean against the mountain sky.

Mother Francesca, the superior of the Schio house, greeted us in the small courtyard, a compact woman of perhaps fifty, with intelligent eyes and a no-nonsense manner.

"Welcome to Schio, Sister Josephine," she said, embracing me with surprising warmth. "We have heard much about you and are grateful for your presence among us."

"Thank you for receiving me, Mother. I come to serve however I may be needed."

She nodded, pleased with this response. "You'll find us a simple community. Seventeen sisters, most local to this region. Our work is with the children of factory workers and farmers, education, basic healthcare, spiritual formation."

She showed me to my cell, a small room similar to what I had left in Venice, though with a window facing east toward the mountains rather than west toward water.

"You'll begin your duties tomorrow," she said. "The children are eager to meet you."

"The children?" I echoed, placing my small bundle of belongings on the narrow bed.

"From our school. Word has spread that a sister from Africa has joined us. They have many questions, as children do."

It was not the first time I had been an object of curiosity, nor would it be the last. Children at least were honest in their wonder.

Sister Giovanna, the senior teacher, showed me the schoolroom the following morning, a large chamber on the ground floor, rows of wooden desks facing a blackboard, shelves of books along one wall, windows overlooking a small vegetable garden.

"Forty-three students, ages six to twelve," she said. "Most from the town, some walking from farms." She ran a hand along one of the desks. "They have been counting the days since we announced your arrival."

"What do they expect of me?" I asked.

A quick flash of mischief crossed her otherwise solemn face. "A princess, perhaps. Or a sorceress."

"I am neither," I said.

"No," she agreed. "But you have an extraordinary story, which might teach them more than all our lessons in geography and history combined."

"When the time is right," I said. "First, let them know me as I am now, not only as what I was before."

The children filed in the next morning in two orderly lines, dark-blue uniforms, white collars, faces scrubbed pink. Their expressions ranged from open curiosity to barely concealed excitement to, in a few cases, something that edged toward apprehension.

Sister Giovanna introduced me with deliberate casualness. Forty-three pairs of eyes fixed on me with an intensity that might have been unnerving had I not endured far more threatening scrutiny in my life. I smiled, letting my gaze move slowly across their young faces.

"*Buongiorno*, children," I said. "I am happy to meet you and to share in your learning."

A small hand shot up at once, a girl of perhaps eight, braids the color of wheat, a sprinkling of freckles across her nose.

"Are you really from Africa?" she asked, the question bursting from her.

A ripple of nervous laughter moved through the room, quickly silenced by Sister Giovanna. I smiled, untroubled.

"Yes. I was born in Sudan, in a village called Olgossa, though I have lived in Italy for many years now."

Another hand, an older boy with serious eyes and a calculating expression. "Is it true that there are lions where you come from?"

"Yes, though I never saw one myself. But I heard them sometimes at night, roaring in the distance."

A stir of excitement. More hands. Questions about animals, weather, food, clothing, how I had come to Italy, why my skin was so dark. I answered each simply and truthfully, omitting the more harrowing details, but not pretending the journey had been other than it was.

"My skin is dark because God made it so," I told one wide-eyed child. "Just as He made yours fair and Sister Giovanna's olive and the sky blue and the grass green. The world is full of colors, all of them beautiful in their way."

By the end of that first morning the initial wariness had largely dissolved. Children have an instinct for authenticity, for detecting whether an adult is genuinely present or merely performing. They seemed to understand that I spoke to them not from condescension but from a real desire to connect.

All except one. A small boy in the last row, dark eyes never meeting mine, body held with the stillness of one trying to avoid notice. When the children were dismissed, he slipped out quickly, avoiding the press of others who crowded around me for a last question or a closer look.

"That is Paolo," said Sister Giovanna when I asked. "He has been with us only a month. His mother died last winter. His father works long hours at the wool factory. Paolo speaks rarely and trusts less."

"I will not press him," I said. "Some wounds must be approached from an angle, if at all."

In the weeks that followed, I settled into Schio's rhythms. The work was more physically demanding than Venice's, the resources more limited, the connection to the surrounding community more immediate. We rose before dawn for prayer, worked through the day in school, infirmary, or garden, and retired early, bodies tired and spirits quiet.

The children brought unexpected pleasure. Their eager minds, their unfiltered questions, their capacity for astonishment, something in me rose to meet all of it. I taught them basic arithmetic and reading, shared stories of Sudan, showed them how to identify birds by their songs, taught them games I remembered from before everything changed. In return they taught me about their mountains, the cycles of planting and harvest in this northern climate, the feast days that marked their year.

In the infirmary, I assisted Sister Teresa in tending to ailments of both the convent community and the townspeople who came for help with minor injuries or illness. My hands, once trained for servitude, had learned over the years how to bandage wounds, prepare herbal remedies, ease pain with the right touch or word.

Three weeks after my arrival, Paolo came to the infirmary. He had fallen during recreation and gashed his knee on a stone. Sister Giovanna brought him to us, the boy white-faced with pain but dry-eyed, lips pressed together in stoic endurance.

"Sister Josephine will tend to you," said Sister Teresa, occupied with an elderly sister suffering from rheumatism. "She has a gentle touch."

Paolo's eyes widened, darting toward me and away, his body tensing. I approached slowly, movements deliberate, voice calm.

"Let me see your knee, Paolo," I said, kneeling to his level rather than standing over him. "I promise to be careful."

He extended his leg reluctantly. A nasty cut, still oozing. I examined it without touching.

"It will need cleaning," I told him. "And perhaps a stitch or two. It will hurt a little, but I will work quickly."

He nodded once, face averted, hands gripping the edge of the bench. I gathered what I needed and set to work.

As I cleansed the wound, his gaze settled on my hands, on the scars marking my wrists and palms, raised patterns against my dark skin. His eyes widened with a different kind of recognition.

"You're hurt too," he said. The first words I had heard from him, barely above a whisper.

I paused in my work. His eyes waited on mine.

"I was," I said. "A long time ago. The marks remain, but they no longer pain me."

He studied my hands, then my face, connecting something. "Who hurt you?"

"People who did not know better," I said after a moment. "People who saw only my usefulness, not my humanity."

His brow furrowed. "Did you cry?"

"Yes. Many times."

"I cry sometimes," he confessed, his voice dropping further. "At night. When no one can hear."

"For your mother?"

A quick jerk of his head. His eyes went bright with unshed tears.

"That is as it should be," I told him, resuming my gentle work. "Tears honor those we have lost. They are nothing to be ashamed of."

He watched in silence as I worked, his body gradually releasing the rigid tension it had held since his arrival. When I tied off the last stitch and began bandaging his knee, he spoke again.

"Does God make bad things happen? Sister Giovanna says God knows everything before it happens. So, He must have known my mother would die. And He must have known you would be hurt."

The question, that ancient, unanswerable question, fell between us with all the weight of a child's directness. I could have offered the standard responses about free will and mystery. But Paolo deserved better than that.

"I don't believe God makes bad things happen," I said carefully. "But He allows us, all of us, to choose good or evil. And sometimes people choose evil, and that choice hurts others. As for your mother's death, illness is part of our world, part of the brokenness that afflicts all creation. God did not want her to die, Paolo. But He was with her when she did, just as He is with you now in your grief."

The boy considered this, his face solemn beyond his years. "How do you know?"

"Because He was with me," I said simply. "In the darkest places, in the worst moments. I did not always recognize His presence. But looking back, I can see it now. The thread of grace that led me from there to here, from then to now."

Paolo nodded slowly, as if this made a kind of sense to him that other answers had not. "Your hands don't scare me anymore," he said.

I smiled. "I'm glad. And your tears don't diminish you in my eyes."

"The little one follows you like a shadow," observed Mother Francesca one evening, as we sat in her office reviewing the week's activities. "He has spoken more in the past month than in all the time before your arrival."

"He is healing," I said.

She nodded, making a note in her ledger. "The others have taken to calling you Madre Moretta. Little Black Mother. Did you know?"

I had not known. The title startled me. Not the word black, which was simply descriptive, but mother, with all it implied of nurture, of fundamental bond, of a love that shapes and sustains.

"I am not their mother," I said. "I am their teacher, their nurse perhaps."

"You are what they need you to be," said Mother Francesca. "As we all are, in God's service. If these children find in you a maternal presence, a source of comfort and guidance, that is a gift to be honored, not denied."

"Madre Moretta," I said, testing the sound of it.

"If it serves them," she said simply, "accept it."

The title spread beyond the school into the wider community of Schio. The townspeople, initially curious about the African nun in their midst, gradually came to know me not as an exotic presence but as a particular kind of servant. One who listened with special attention to children's concerns, who told stories that transported listeners beyond the confines of their valley, who bore in her body the visible marks of suffering that had not broken her.

Not all the children came to me with equal ease. There were some, particularly among the older boys, who regarded my dark skin with suspicion. Others were drawn close at first, then recoiled upon glimpsing my scars.

One such child was Lucia, a delicate girl of ten with enormous blue eyes and a nervous disposition. She had shown real interest in my stories of Sudan, asking thoughtful questions about the animals and plants of my homeland. But one afternoon, as I reached to help her adjust her grip on a pen, my sleeve pulled back slightly, revealing the scar pattern on my forearm.

She gasped and jerked away so sharply she knocked her inkwell to the floor, where it shattered in a spray of blue-black across the wooden planks.

"Lucia!" exclaimed Sister Giovanna.

The girl stood frozen, eyes fixed on my arm, face drained of color. "Her skin," she whispered. "It's marked. Like the pictures of demons in Father Matteo's book."

A hush fell over the classroom. I pulled my sleeve down calmly.

"Not demons, Lucia," I said gently. "Just scars. Marks left by people who did unkind things many years ago."

Her eyes remained wide. "But they're patterns. Not like when Giovanni fell and cut his arm. They look — made."

"They were made," I acknowledged. "By people who wanted to mark me as their property. But I am not property, Lucia. I am a person, just as you are. These marks are part of my history. They do not define who I am now."

Sister Giovanna moved closer, her presence steady beside me. "Sister Josephine has shared with you the beauty of her homeland, the games she played as a child, the animals she knew. Today she shares something harder but equally important, that human beings can be cruel to one another, and that such cruelty need not have the final word."

Lucia's enormous eyes filled, then the tears spilled at once, two straight lines down her pale cheeks. Her mouth pressed flat, as though she were holding something in that had become too large to contain. She looked from my sleeve to my face and then to the ink spreading slowly across the floor.

"Did it hurt?" she asked finally.

"Yes. Very much."

"And now?"

"Now it is a memory. A scar, not a wound."

She looked at the shattered inkwell, the blue-black spreading slowly between us. "I'm sorry I broke it," she whispered.

"It's only ink," I said. "It can be cleaned up. Some messes are more easily resolved than others."

The following morning, Lucia appeared before lessons began, her face solemn but no longer afraid. She held out a small package wrapped in a handkerchief.

"For you, Sister," she said.

Inside was a small clay figure, crudely shaped but recognizable. A woman in a habit, her face and hands painted dark against the black of her robes.

"It's you," said Lucia. "My father helped me make it. I told him about you, about your scars, about what you said. He said you must be very brave."

I looked from the figure to the child's face. Something opened in my chest. A warmth without a name that felt like gratitude, like recognition.

"Thank you, Lucia," I said. "I will treasure it."

I placed the small clay figure on the windowsill of my cell that evening, where the morning light would find it first. Outside the window the mountains held their position against the darkening sky, solid and unhurried. Below, the town settled into its evening quiet. A door closing, a child called in, the last bell of the day rolling across the rooftops and out into the surrounding hills until the sound was gone.

Chapter Sixteen

By January the mountains were gone. Not truly gone, they stood where they had always stood, but the cloud had taken them, and what remained in their place was a white opacity that pressed down on the town from all sides, making Schio feel smaller, more enclosed, the streets between the convent and the wool factory narrower than they had been in autumn.

I had been in Schio for five months.

Five months of being Madre Moretta to the children, of earning the townspeople's cautious respect, of adjusting to this northern place so unlike Venice's watery labyrinth or Sudan's burning plains. Five months of a new life that felt increasingly like my own rather than one assigned to me, of roots beginning to take hold in foreign soil.

And then, on the Feast of the Epiphany, the dreams returned.

They came without warning, erupting through the fragile membrane that had separated my present from my past. I dreamed of the slave market in Khartoum, the particular stench of fear and unwashed bodies, the sound of chains dragging across packed earth, the precise weight of a stranger's assessing gaze on my naked skin. I dreamed of the branding house, the knives heated to glowing, the iron's touch that turned the world white with pain, the smell of my flesh burning. I dreamed of the Turkish officer's wife, her cane finding my back with terrible accuracy.

I woke drenched in sweat despite the January cold, not knowing for a moment where I was. Not Venice, certainly not Sudan, but this small cell with its window now framing nothing but white. The disorientation lasted longer than it should have, leaving me sitting upright in the dark with my hands pressed flat against the mattress, waiting for the room to become certain again.

The dreams continued, night after night. Sometimes I woke before the worst moments. Other times I remained trapped in memory until the nightmare had run its full course, leaving me hollowed by dawn.

Sister Margherita, whose cell adjoined mine, heard me one night, not screaming, for I had learned long ago the value of silent suffering, but praying in a voice made strange by terror, words from my childhood tongue mixing with Italian supplications.

"Sister Josephine," she whispered, appearing at my door in her nightdress, her face creased with concern. "Are you unwell?"

I sat on the edge of my bed, the sheets twisted around my legs, my nightdress damp with sweat. "Dreams," I said simply. "Nothing to trouble yourself over."

She did not press. The following day I found a small sachet of dried lavender on my pillow, a remedy for restless sleep. Her kindness touched me, though the lavender proved no match for the ghosts that stalked my nights.

A week after the dreams began, Mother Francesca summoned me to her office. Winter light fell through her window in pale shafts. She sat at her desk; hands folded atop the leather-bound volume I recognized as the convent's official chronicle.

"You look tired, Sister Josephine," she said without preamble.

"I am well enough," I replied with the standard response expected of us in religious life, where personal comfort was never to take precedence over duty.

Her eyes assessed me with dispassionate precision. "Sister Margherita reports that you have been troubled by dreams."

Something tightened in my chest. Not anger at the perceived disclosure, but the vulnerability of having one's private sufferings exposed to view. "They will pass," I said. "They always do."

"This has happened before?"

"Yes. Periodically. Periods of remembering."

She nodded. "The past is persistent." She tapped the leather volume before her. "Do you know what this is?"

"The convent chronicle."

"Yes. The official record of our community's life, its works, its challenges, its notable members." She opened it, turning pages slowly. "I have been in correspondence with your former superior in Venice. She mentioned that you have never provided a complete account of your experiences before coming to Italy. That your testimony, while powerful, has always been selective."

The observation struck an uncomfortable chord. In all my years of speaking about my past, I had shared enough to illustrate God's redeeming power, enough to educate about slavery's horrors, but never the complete narrative in its most intimate brutality.

"Some details serve no purpose in testimony," I said carefully. "They would only turn attention to the sensational rather than the spiritual."

"Perhaps," she conceded. "But there is another purpose beyond testimony to others. There is the matter of preserving the truth for those who come after us. The full truth, not merely its palatable portions."

She closed the chronicle and looked at me directly. "I am asking you, Sister Josephine, to write your story. Not for publication, not for sharing beyond these walls unless you choose, but for the record. For yourself. For God."

The request fell between us. Write my story , not speak it in measured doses, not hint at it in discreet allusions, but commit it to paper in all its terrible detail.

"I am not a writer," I said.

"You write beautifully in your journal. Sister Fabretti spoke highly of your progress. This would be no different. Simply a longer narrative, a more complete accounting."

"And if I prefer not to revisit those memories?"

"They are already revisiting you," she said, her voice gentle but unyielding. "These dreams. They come uninvited, uncontrolled. Perhaps in writing, in choosing which memories to engage and when, you might find a different relationship with them."

I could not argue with the logic of her words, though something in me recoiled from the task she proposed. To write would mean to remember deliberately, to summon what I had spent years trying to transcend.

"I will consider it," I said.

She nodded. "Take as long as you need. The past will wait. It always does."

But it did not wait. That night the dreams came again with redoubled intensity, as if Mother Francesca's request had unlocked doors in my mind that had been kept deliberately shut. I dreamed of the forest where I had been taken, the exact quality of light through leaves, the precise sound of my sister's scream, the moment before the slavers emerged from the trees. I dreamed of the desert crossing, the weight of chains against raw skin. I dreamed of the first time I was sold, standing in the market while men examined my teeth, my limbs, my body as though I were livestock being assessed for purchase.

I awoke in the coldest hour before dawn. The cell was dark save for a thin sliver of moonlight across the bed. In that pale light I looked at my hands, darker than the shadows, scarred, but steady, no longer the hands of a slave but of a woman who had chosen her own life.

Hands that could, perhaps, write the story that haunted her.

I rose, lit my small lamp, and sat at the desk. From the drawer I withdrew my journal. I turned to the final blank pages, took up my pen, and wrote.

I was not born a slave.

The words appeared on the page in my careful script, black against white, definitive as judgment. I stared at them.

> *I was born free, the daughter of a family whose name I no longer remember, in a village called Olgossa that may no longer exist. I had a mother who sang while grinding millet, a father whose shoulders carried me above thickets of tall grass, sisters whose laughter mingled with birdsong in my earliest memories.*

My hand moved across the page with growing confidence, the pen's scratching the only sound in the pre-dawn stillness. I wrote until the bell rang for morning prayer, filling three pages with the beginning of my story, not the horrors that would come later, but the life that had preceded them, the humanity that had been mine by birthright before it was denied me by force.

That afternoon I sought Mother Francesca in the garden, where she was supervising the pruning of dormant rose bushes whose bare canes stood black and angular against the snow.

"I have begun," I told her.

She nodded, understanding immediately. "Good. I will adjust your duties accordingly. Fewer hours in the classroom. None in the infirmary for the time being."

"That isn't necessary," I protested. "I can write in the evenings."

"This is your responsibility now," she said. "This reckoning with your past. We serve God not merely through external works, but through the internal work of truth-telling."

I bowed my head, accepting.

"I will need paper," I said. "More than my journal provides."

"Of course. You shall have the small room next to the library. Private, undisturbed, with a proper desk and better light."

The arrangements were made swiftly. By the following day I had been installed in a small chamber, once a nun's cell, since repurposed for storage, containing a sturdy desk beneath a narrow window, a straight-backed chair, a small bookshelf of reference texts, and a brazier against the January cold. Mother Francesca brought me blank paper, a new bottle of ink, and several fresh nibs.

"Take the mornings for your writing," she instructed. "The light is best then. You will still assist Sister Giovanna with the children in the afternoons, but for reduced hours."

"What if I cannot find the words?" I asked.

"They will come," she said. "The story is already written in you. You need only transcribe it."

That night, sleep came mercifully free of dreams. I woke at dawn clearheaded, made my way to the writing room after Mass and a simple breakfast, arranged my materials with careful precision, and sat before the blank sheet.

Then stared at it.

Where to begin? With my earliest memories of Olgossa, as I had in my journal? With the raid? The first sale? The succession of masters? The journey to Italy?

My life was not a neat narrative. It was a tangle of memories, some so vivid the smell of them returned with the recollection, others faded beyond recovery, still others missing entirely, lost to trauma or the simple passage of time. The pen grew heavy in my hand. The page held its silence.

I set the pen down, closed my eyes, and did the only thing I knew when faced with an impossible task: I prayed. Not the formal prayers of the Divine Office, but the wordless reaching of a soul toward its Creator.

In that stillness, a memory surfaced, one that was not about the violence, but of my mother teaching me to grind grain between stones. The precise pressure needed. The circular motion. The gradual transformation of hard kernels into flour. *"Patience,"* she had said, her voice so clear it might have been yesterday rather than decades ago. *"The grain does not become flour all at once. Each turn of the stone, each moment of pressure, that is how transformation happens."*

I took up the pen and wrote.

> *My mother's hands were strong and certain on the grinding stone. "Like this," she would say, guiding my small hands to join hers in the circular motion that would transform millet into flour. "Patience, daughter. The grain does not become flour all at once."*
>
> *I did not understand then that she was teaching me not just how to grind grain, but how to endure, how to continue applying pressure when results are not immediate, how to trust in processes of transformation that require time and persistence.*
>
> *This knowledge would serve me well in the years to come, though neither of us could have imagined the particular kind of grinding that awaited me, the pressure that would attempt to reduce me not to nourishing flour, but to nothing at all, to an object without will or worth or identity.*

The words flowed from there, one memory leading to another in the associative pattern of actual recollection. From my mother's lesson at the grinding stone, I moved to the day of the raid, the silence that fell in the forest, the way the birds had ceased their singing, the expression on my sister's face in the moment before the slavers emerged from the trees.

I wrote steadily until the convent bells rang for midday prayer, filling several pages. The work left me drained and oddly alert, the way the body feels after labor that has asked for everything and received it.

After prayers and the simple midday meal, I joined Sister Giovanna in the classroom where the children were practicing their letters, small heads bent over slates, the scratch of chalk the only sound in the concentrated silence. I moved among them, correcting a grip here, praising a well-formed letter there.

"You seem far away today, Madre Moretta," said Paolo. He sat in the third row, dark eyes steady on my face with the perception of the deeply wounded.

"Not far away," I replied, smiling to soften the correction. "Just thinking of many things."

"About Africa?" he asked, lowering his voice so the others would not hear.

"Yes. About my childhood there."

"Was it very different from here?" He gestured toward the window, where snow had fallen again, transforming the schoolyard into unbroken white.

"As different as day from night," I said. "The heat, the colors, the smells, all unlike anything you have known."

"Will you tell us about it?" His question was eager, innocent, unaware of the cost that remembering now carried.

I looked at his slate, neat, careful script that revealed both intelligence and discipline. "Perhaps someday," I said. "But first I must write it down, so I can tell it properly."

He nodded with the patient hope of a child accepting an adult's someday. "I would like to read it when you finish," he said.

"We shall see," I replied.

That evening, in the weekly audience Mother Francesca had established between us, I expressed what had been growing in me all afternoon.

"Certain memories arise that seem too intimate, too harsh for others to read," I said. "Yet if I omit them, the account will be dishonest in its selectivity."

She considered this, her face grave in the lamplight. "For whom are you writing, Sister Josephine?"

The question stopped me. "For the record," I replied. "For the convent chronicles."

She waited, saying nothing more.

The silence stretched. I sat with the question, turning it slowly, and something clarified, not her answer but my own.

"For the girl I was," I said finally. "Who had no voice, no witness. For her."

Mother Francesca nodded once. "Then you know what you must write."

"I must write everything," I said. "The moments of greatest degradation. The pain. The violations that left no visible mark." I heard my own voice say the words and understood them as I spoke them. "All of it."

"Yes," she agreed. "Though not all at once. Begin where you can, with what you can bear today. The writing will show you the way forward."

"It will not be easy," I said.

"Few worthwhile things are," she replied.

We agreed that each Friday I would bring her what I had written during the week. She would read it in my presence or absence, as I preferred, and we would speak of it only if I wished to do so.

That night the dreams came again, but differently. I dreamed of the branding house, the Turkish officer's cellar, the desert march, but alongside the experiencing of these things, something else was present. A watching. A steadiness that had not been there before.

I woke before dawn, dressed in the dark, and went to the writing room without waiting for the bell. The mountains were invisible still, the window showing only the grey white of cloud pressing close. I lit the lamp, sat at the desk, and opened the leather portfolio.

The page from the previous day's work lay on top. I read the last line I had written, the moment of the raid, my sister's face, the forest going still, and took up the pen.

> *The journey from my village to the slave market took seventeen days. Seventeen days of walking until my feet bled, of thirst that turned my tongue to leather, of learning that human beings could be treated as less than animals and that those doing the treating did not consider themselves cruel.*

I wrote until my hand cramped around the pen, until the bells called us to prayer, until the lamp's oil ran low and the winter light had risen enough to write by without it.

Near the bottom of the page I stopped. Read back what I had written. Then, in the clearer hand I used for things I wished to keep, I added a single line beneath the rest.

> *I was not born a slave. I will not die one.*

The bell began outside, its sound crossing the rooftops and moving out toward the cloud-covered hills. I sat with the words a moment longer, the ink still wet on the page. Then I capped the ink, set down the pen, and went to join the sisters for morning prayer.

Chapter Seventeen

The writing consumed me.

Day after day I returned to the small room with its narrow window and desk, filling page after page with memories excavated from depths I had long sealed against examination. Each morning, I descended further into my past. Each afternoon, I emerged into the present, blinking, off-balance, the way one feels stepping from a dark room into open air. The children noticed a new remoteness, a shadow behind my eyes that had not been there before. Paolo watched me with the solemn attention of one who recognizes suffering in its many forms.

"You look tired, Madre Moretta," he said one afternoon as I helped him with his arithmetic. The other children had gone to the yard for recreation, but he had stayed behind, ostensibly to complete unfinished work.

"I am well enough," I replied with the same answer I gave to all inquiries.

"My father looks like that sometimes," he continued, his pencil motionless on the slate. "When he remembers my mother. Like he's seeing something that isn't there."

I could not deny what he so clearly recognized.

"I am remembering," I admitted, my voice low. "Things from long ago. It is necessary, but not easy."

He nodded, his face grave beyond his years. "The bad things?"

"Yes. The bad things."

"Does it help? To remember?"

I considered his question with the seriousness it deserved. Three weeks of writing now. Three weeks of naming horrors I had endured but never fully articulated. Three weeks of approaching the desk each morning with increasing dread, of returning to my cell each night stripped of something I could not immediately name.

"I don't yet know," I said. "But sometimes we must face darkness before we can fully appreciate light."

He accepted this. "I could help you," he offered. "I could read to you from the books Sister Giovanna gives us. Stories with happy endings."

The offer touched me, its innocent presumption that happiness was available to all stories if only they continued long enough. "That is very kind," I said. "Perhaps sometime soon."

But soon did not come. As I progressed deeper into the narrative, past the initial kidnapping, past the desert crossing, into the succession of masters and the brutalities each had visited upon me, a weight settled on my spirit that prayer did not lighten, that communion did not dissolve.

Mother Francesca had been reading my pages each Friday as promised, her face steady as she turned each leaf, her eyes the only indication of her response, widening occasionally, filling once with tears she did not shed, darkening at certain passages with something that might have been anger. She never interrupted, never offered comfort or expressions of horror. She simply read, witnessing my past with the attention of one who understands that some burdens are lightened by being seen rather than diminished.

On the fourth Friday, after reading the section detailing my time in the branding house, the knives heated to glowing, the salt rubbed into fresh cuts, the precise smell of my flesh being altered against my will, she set the pages down and looked at me directly.

"Your writing has changed," she observed.

I waited.

"The earlier pages held pain but also perspective, the voice of the woman you have become reflecting on the girl you were. These last pages are different. As if the distance has collapsed."

Her perception was uncomfortably exact. What had begun as testimony was becoming something else. A reliving, a reopening of wounds I had thought scarred over.

"It is difficult material," I said.

"Yes. But there is something beyond difficulty here." She tapped the last page. "You write, 'God was not present in that room. There was only pain, only masters, only the reduction of a human being to an object to be marked at will.'" She looked up. "Do you believe that? That God was absent from your suffering?"

The question struck with unexpected force. Throughout my years of testimony, I had spoken of God's presence across my journey, the thread of grace discernible looking backward, the divine hand recognizable in my deliverance. It was the redemptive arc that made my story bearable to those who heard it.

But immersed now in the unvarnished reality of what had been done to me, that certainty wavered. Where had God been when they carved patterns into my flesh? Where had divine justice been when my sister was struck down before my eyes, when everything human in me was systematically stripped away?

"I don't know," I said, the admission feeling like betrayal. "I want to believe He was there. I have built my life upon that belief. But in the writing, when I return to those moments completely, I cannot sense His presence."

Mother Francesca nodded, neither surprised nor troubled by this confession from a woman under solemn vows. "The dark night of the soul comes to many who walk the path of faith," she said. "Often to those who have known the greatest suffering. Even Christ cried out in abandonment on the cross."

"But Christ knew why He suffered," I replied, the words carrying an edge I had not intended. "His pain had purpose, meaning. What purpose could there have been in the suffering of a child who had done nothing to deserve such treatment? What meaning in the systematic destruction of dignity, of selfhood? What divine plan required such cruelty?"

She did not flinch at the implicit accusation in my questions. "I cannot answer that," she said simply. "No one can, this side of eternity. But doubt is not sin, Sister Josephine. Questioning is not faithlessness. Sometimes it is the most honest form of prayer."

That night, as I knelt for evening prayer in the chapel, the weight that had been accumulating over weeks of remembering crystallized into something harder and colder. For the first time since my profession, I could not pray. The words of the familiar devotions turned to ash, empty syllables shaped by habit rather than conviction. The crucifix above the altar, which had once spoken to me of love's triumph over suffering, now seemed merely a depiction of torture, one victim among countless others whose pain served no discernible purpose in a world of random cruelty.

I remained on my knees long after the other sisters had departed, long after the chapel had fallen into darkness broken only by the perpetual flame before the tabernacle. The devotion that had sustained me through earlier trials was not there. The presence I had once found as real and intimate as breath. That too was gone.

Only silence. Only the cold press of stone beneath my knees and a darker cold spreading through my spirit.

Back in my cell, I lay on the narrow bed watching moonlight cross the wall. Outside, the wind moved around the stone corners of the convent. The mountains beyond my window rose black against the star-strewn sky.

In that restless darkness, the doubts that had been gathering through weeks of writing coalesced into a voice. Not audible, not external, but distinct within my mind as if another consciousness had taken up residence beside my own.

What kind of God allows children to be enslaved? What kind of divine love permits innocent flesh to be branded, innocent spirits to be broken? You have wasted your life serving a God who abandoned you when you needed Him most. Your faith is built on desperate illusion — the need to create meaning where there is none. There was no divine plan in your suffering, no thread of grace through your torment. There was only human cruelty and your own stubborn will to survive it.

I rose from the bed, took up my rosary, the beads smooth against my fingers, worn by years of use, and began the first decade, my lips forming the Ave Maria. But the voice continued beneath the ritual words.

Think of the others. The millions still in chains. The children still being taken. Where is God for them? Why should you alone have been delivered while countless others remain captive? What kind of justice is so arbitrary in its distribution of mercy?

Memories rose. Not the distant ones I had been writing about, but others. The man on the slave block in Khartoum whose eyes had met mine briefly before he was dragged away. The woman in the Turkish officer's household who had died under the lash for a minor infraction. The child in the merchant's compound who had simply vanished one night, never spoken of again.

What had become of them? Had they found deliverance as I had? Or had they died as they had lived, as property, as tools, as things rather than persons?

The rosary slipped from my fingers, the beads scattering across the floor. I sank to my knees in a kind of collapse, my arms wrapped around myself as if to hold together something that threatened to come apart entirely.

I do not know how long I knelt there. The night seemed to stretch without motion. My body ached from the stone floor. The voice of doubt had, for the moment, exhausted itself, and in its wake came not peace but a vast and ringing emptiness.

Then something changed in the quality of the darkness.

The air acquired a different quality. It was not warmer exactly, but present in a way it had not been. A scent entered the room, unlike incense or any earthly fragrance, something wilder and quieter at once, the way certain evenings carry the smell of things about to bloom.

The moonlight had shifted. Or not shifted, but changed in quality, as though the cold light of reflection had acquired a faint warmth from within.

A figure stood in the cell. She had not entered through the door. She was simply there, in the way that certain certainties are simply there, appearing without warning, but recognized.

She was robed in blue so deep it was almost black. Her face was neither European nor African, but something that encompassed both, dark as turned earth, composed, with a stillness that was not the stillness of absence but of absolute presence. Around her head, faint light moved the way candlelight moves in a room with no draught.

No words were spoken. None were needed.

She did not erase my questions. She did not answer them. She simply stood, and her standing was itself a kind of answer, not to the arguments that had driven me to the floor, but to the need beneath them: the need to know that suffering, however complete, is witnessed. That abandonment, however absolute it seems in the depths of a winter night, is never the final truth.

The figure faded the way the last light fades, gradually, without a single moment of departure. And I was alone again on the stone floor, my face wet, the scattered rosary beads around my knees.

I gathered the beads from the floor, restringing them slowly, one by one. When the rosary was whole again, I held it without praying. Outside the window the mountains were becoming visible. The cloud had lifted in the night, and the first grey of dawn was separating their peaks from the sky.

The questions were still there. They had not dissolved with the vision. Doubt was still present at the edges of the morning's quiet, residual, waiting. But something in me had shifted, not from uncertainty to certainty, but from the brittle defensiveness of threatened faith toward something steadier and less easily broken. A faith that did not require the absence of question. A faith that could hold the darkness without being extinguished by it.

When the bell rang for morning prayer, I joined the other sisters in the chapel, my face composed though my eyes showed I had not slept. I knelt beside those who had no knowledge of what had passed in my cell through the night. I spoke the familiar words of the morning prayers, my voice joining theirs.

Later that day, I returned to the writing room. The pages of suffering waited. I sat at the desk, took up my pen, and wrote, not as one who has been given answers, but as one who has been given something else: the steadiness to keep asking.

Where was God during the branding? I do not know with the certainty I once claimed. Perhaps in the air that filled my lungs even as I screamed. Perhaps in the darkness that finally claimed me when pain exceeded endurance. Perhaps in the quiet resistance that remained within me even as my body was marked against my will.

Perhaps God was present not as the powerful intervener I longed for, but as the fellow sufferer I did not recognize, the one who had also been stripped, beaten, treated as less than human by those who could not see the divine image in the vulnerable flesh before them.

Perhaps God's silence was not absence but a deeper form of presence. The presence that does not explain suffering or prevent it but enters fully into it, transforms it from within, ensures that it cannot have the final word in any human story, including mine.

I do not know. I may never know in this life. But after a night of deepest doubt, I choose again to believe, not with the brittle certainty of one who has never questioned, but with the hard-won trust of one who has faced the abyss and discovered, even there, the possibility of light.

I set the pen down. Outside the window, snow had begun to fall, quiet, unhurried, covering the winter-bare garden in white. I watched it settle on the dormant earth and did not move to close the shutter. The cold that entered was clean and sharp, carrying the mineral scent of altitude.

I took up the pen again and continued.

Chapter Eighteen

Spring came reluctantly to Schio that year. March winds blew cold from the mountains, and the convent garden still slept, buds sealed against late frosts, the earth not yet ready to give. Only the snowdrops had come, small and white along the wall, their stems bending in the wind but not breaking.

I had been in Schio for five months.

"You are not paying attention to my words, Sister Josephine," said Mother Francesca, her voice cutting through my distraction. We sat in her office reviewing my narrative, which now filled a thick leather folder.

"Forgive me," I replied, drawing my attention back to her. "I find myself tired lately."

Her eyes narrowed. "You look unwell. How long have you had that cough?"

The cough, a small, persistent rattle in my chest since winter, had become so constant I had ceased to notice it. "It is nothing," I said. "Left over from the cold we all had in February."

"And the weight you have lost? Is that also nothing?"

I had noticed my habit hanging more loosely, my collarbones more prominent when I fastened my head covering each morning. I had blamed it on

Lenten fasting, on the physical demands of teaching while continuing to write, on the natural process of a body now nearing fifty. "I am well enough," I said.

Mother Francesca's expression showed rare frustration. "Sister Josephine, your entire life story speaks of the sacred dignity of physical existence. Yet you treat your own body as irrelevant to your work."

The observation landed uncomfortably close to the truth. Since beginning to record my experiences, I had treated my physical self as little more than a vehicle for memory and testimony, pushing through tiredness, dismissing the increasing pain that bloomed along my nerves and joints.

"I will rest more," I promised.

"You will see Sister Teresa in the infirmary," she replied. "Today, after your duties with the children are complete. That is not a suggestion."

The infirmary was warmed by a small stove, the air carrying the mingled scents of herbal remedies and cleaning soap. Sister Teresa looked up from her record book as I entered, set down her pen, and gestured to the examining table.

"Remove your head covering and collar," she said, approaching with the practiced confidence of decades of service. "I need to examine your throat and neck."

Her hands were gentle but thorough as she found swelling invisible to the eye. She listened to my breathing with her stethoscope, the metal disk cold against my back.

"How long have you been having night sweats?" she asked.

“Some weeks,” I admitted. “Perhaps longer.”

“And the pain in your joints? When did that begin?”

I looked at her in surprise. I had mentioned no such pain, had been hiding it even from myself, dismissing the ache in my knees and hips and shoulders as the result of hours bent over my writing desk.

“Your movements give you away,” she said. “The way you favor your right side. The stiffness when you rise from prayer. The slight wince when the children embrace you too enthusiastically.”

I had not realized my discomfort was so visible. “It comes and goes,” I said. “It is manageable.”

She continued her examination methodically. When she reached my forearm, where the geometric scars from the branding house remained visible after all these years, she paused.

“How long has this area been inflamed?” Her finger hovered just above the scar tissue, the skin reddened, slightly swollen, warmer than the surrounding flesh.

“It has always been sensitive,” I said, drawing my arm back.

She held my wrist, preventing escape. “This is not sensitivity. This is active inflammation. Are there other places where your old wounds have reasserted themselves?”

I hesitated. I had noticed the pattern for months and ignored it, Certain scars becoming tender, occasionally weeping clear fluid, as if the original injuries were working their way back to the surface after decades of apparent healing. “My back,” I admitted. “And here.” I touched my collarbone. “But it is not important. Old wounds sometimes remember themselves.”

Sister Teresa’s face remained professional, but her eyes held concern. “Many of these show signs of renewed inflammation,” she said finally, helping me to dress. "As if your body is fighting old battles, reopening wounds long supposedly healed."

"Is that possible?" I asked. "For scars to reactivate after so many years?"

"The body has its own memory," she said carefully. "Sometimes physical trauma remains stored within tissues long after visible healing appears complete. And when the mind returns to those traumatic experiences—" She did not finish the thought. We both understood the connection between my writing and this rebellion of my flesh.

"Rest," she said. "A pause in your writing. Better nourishment, more sleep, reduced hours in the classroom. And I will prepare a salve for these inflamed areas."

I nodded, knowing I could not fully comply. The writing had acquired its own necessity. To abandon it halfway would be to leave the testimony incomplete, the journey through darkness stopped before whatever light waited on the far side.

"I will speak with Mother Francesca," Sister Teresa continued.

"Please," I said, more urgently than I had intended. "The children should not be frightened by concerns about my health."

"I will be discreet," she said. "But I must be honest with her about what I have observed."

I left with a small jar of salve, instructions to return in three days, and the uncomfortable awareness that my body was betraying what my composed manner had concealed.

A week later, Mother Francesca called me to her office with news she described as unexpected.

"People have been asking for you," she said. "Not just the children or their parents, but others from the town. Those who have heard of Madre Moretta, whose stories have awakened curiosity or connected with their own sufferings."

"What do they want from me?" I asked.

"Various things. A woman whose husband is abusive has asked if you might speak with her. A man who lost his arm in a factory accident wonders how you have made peace with bodily suffering. A couple whose child died of fever last winter seeks comfort from one who has known great loss."

I sat with the list of ordinary human pain, different from the extraordinary brutality I had endured, yet no less real to those experiencing it.

"You believe I should meet with these people?" I asked. "That I have something to offer them?"

"I believe your experiences, both of suffering and of finding meaning beyond suffering, have given you a particular wisdom that others recognize and seek. Whether you share that wisdom is a decision I leave to your judgment."

"I have no training in spiritual direction," I said. "No education in counselling the afflicted."

"No," she agreed. "Only the education of experience. Which can be more valuable than any formal training."

The possibility was strange and unexpected, that the very wounds now reasserting themselves physically might serve as credentials for a different ministry, that the suffering which seemed to consume me might be transformed into something useful to others.

"I will see them," I said. "If you believe it appropriate."

Mother Francesca nodded, neither surprised nor particularly pleased, as if she had merely been confirming what she already knew would happen. "You will receive visitors in the small parlor near the chapel. For no more than two hours each afternoon. Your health remains a primary concern."

She rose to return to her duties, then paused at the door. "I will inform the family from Padua that their daughter may come. Though I will make clear that expectations of miraculous cures are inappropriate."

I smiled at this. "I promise not to raise the dead or make the lame walk."

"See that you don't," she replied dryly. "Miracles create far too much paperwork for a convent our size to handle efficiently."

They came hesitantly at first. One or two each afternoon, sitting in silence for long minutes before finding words for what had brought them to seek a foreign nun with dark skin and a reputation for having survived what seemed unsurvivable.

A young mother whose child had been born with twisted limbs wept as she spoke of neighbors who crossed themselves when she passed, of her own moments of despair in the night. "How do you bear it?" she asked. "Knowing your body will never be as others' are?"

"I do not bear it perfectly," I said. "There are days when the scars seem heavier than others. But I have learned to see them differently over time, not just as marks of what was done to me, but as testimony to what could not be taken: my humanity, my capacity to love."

"Your scars can be covered," she protested. "My son will never be seen first as himself, always as his twisted limbs."

"Then it is the vision of others that is twisted," I said, the words emerging with more force than I had intended. "Your son is exactly who he is meant to be. Complete, beloved, made in God's image not despite his differences, but including them."

An elderly man came one Wednesday; his hands gnarled from decades in the quarries. He had lost his wife the previous winter and was increasingly drawn toward death, tired of a world that no longer held her presence. "How did you resist it?" he asked. "The temptation?"

"One breath at a time," I said. "One moment lived fully, then another. Not denying the pain, but allowing it to accompany me without defining me. And looking for the small mercies that persist even in deepest grief, the kindness of a neighbor, the memories that pain us precisely because they were born of love."

He nodded slowly, as if recognizing a truth he had known but forgotten. "She loved the spring," he said, his voice softening. "The crocuses especially. They are blooming now in the churchyard where she rests."

"Then perhaps you might visit them," I suggested. "Not to escape your grief, but to honor it, and her."

The girl from Padua came in early June. She was perhaps sixteen, thin to the point of starvation, her eyes enormous in a face drained of color. She did not speak as her father explained her condition, the gradual withdrawal from all normal activities, the refusal of food, the night terrors that left her screaming but unable to name what pursued her through dreams.

When her parents had finished, I asked to speak with their daughter alone. They agreed with visible reluctance.

When we were alone, I did not immediately speak. I sat present to her suffering, creating space for whatever might emerge in the silence between us. She remained motionless, her gaze fixed on her lap, her breathing shallow.

"You need not speak," I said finally, keeping my voice gentle but matter-of-fact. "Words are not always the best carriers of truth, especially truths that live in the body rather than the mind."

She looked up then, a brief, darting glance that carried both terror and something like recognition.

"I understand something of what it means to be wounded," I said, deliberately rolling back my sleeve to reveal the geometric scar pattern on my forearm. "To carry marks others cannot see or choose not to acknowledge. To have one's body become a site of violation rather than sanctuary."

Her eyes fixed on the scarred flesh. Her breathing changed, slightly deeper, slightly slower.

"Someone hurt you," I said. Not a question. A statement of what seemed suddenly, blindingly clear. "Not doctors with their medicines, not melancholy with its darkness, but someone with hands and will and strength greater than yours. Someone who should have protected, but instead harmed."

A single tear tracked down her pale cheek. She did not speak, but her body confessed what her lips could not, a slight trembling of hands, arms crossing over her chest as if to shield herself from an expected blow.

"You need not name them," I said, keeping my voice steady. "Those details belong to you, to reveal or keep hidden as it serves your healing. But know this:

what happened was not your fault. The shame belongs to the one who harmed, not to the one who was harmed."

More tears now, her shoulders beginning to shake with the effort of containing a flood long dammed. I did not move to comfort her physically. Touch, I understood, would be neither welcome nor helpful to one whose boundaries had been so deeply violated. Instead, I sat in witness, creating space for her grief and rage and terror to be acknowledged in their devastating reality.

"I wanted to die," she whispered. The first words she had spoken, so faint I leaned forward to catch them. "I still want to die sometimes."

"Yes," I said simply. "I understand that desire."

She looked at me fully then, her gaze direct for the first time. "Did you? Want to die?"

"Yes. Many times during my captivity, during the worst abuses. And sometimes after, when freedom brought its own terrors, the responsibility to choose, to build, to become something more than what had been done to me."

"How did you not do it?" she asked. "Not die?"

The question deserved more than platitudes about God's plan. "Partly stubbornness," I said, offering my own experience rather than generalized wisdom. "Refusing to grant my abusers that final victory. Partly hope, not the bright, easy hope of the untested, but the stubborn insistence on the possibility of light even in deepest darkness. And partly grace: moments of unexpected beauty or kindness that arrived precisely when most needed, suggesting a world beyond the one defined by cruelty."

She absorbed this, her face solemn with consideration. "I don't know if I'm strong enough," she admitted. "To live with this."

"Strength is not what you think," I told her. "Not the absence of weakness or the capacity to proceed without stumbling. But the willingness to take the next step despite full awareness of one's vulnerability."

We continued for perhaps half an hour more, I speaking, she occasionally responding, the space between us slowly changing in quality, as rooms do when windows are opened after long winter. When I could sense my strength ebbing and her parents' anxiety building outside the door, I made a single suggestion.

"If you are willing," I said, "I would like to write to you. Not often, my health does not allow extensive correspondence. But perhaps once a month. A letter you need not answer if writing proves too difficult, but which might serve as reminder that you are not alone."

She nodded, a quick movement. "I would like that," she whispered.

As she rose to leave, I offered a brief, silent prayer, not a formal declaration, but a simple giving: *Lord, I offer whatever suffering comes to me this day for this child's healing. Use it as You will.*

The visitors continued throughout April and into May, their numbers gradually increasing as word spread through the town of the African sister who listened without judgment, who recognized pain without being destroyed by it, who offered not platitudes but the simple dignity of witness.

In late May, Mother Francesca joined me in the garden where I sat drawing warmth into my perpetually cold limbs. Spring had finally established its claim, roses beginning their first flush, herbs lush in their neat beds.

"The word has spread beyond our town," she said. "I received a letter from the family in Padua. The girl is eating again."

I received this quietly.

"I am concerned about the demands this places upon you," she continued, "given Sister Teresa's reports of your continuing physical decline."

"I have been thinking," I said, "about what seems to happen in these exchanges. As my body weakens, something else appears to strengthen: a capacity to be present to others' pain without being overwhelmed by it. To bear witness to both the reality of darkness and the greater reality of light beyond it."

She was quiet for a moment. A bee moved from blossom to blossom on the nearby rosebush, its industry unhurried and purposeful.

"And the visitors?" she asked finally. "You believe they benefit from this?"

"They seem to," I said. "Not because I offer solutions or particular wisdom, but because in seeing one who has traveled through fire and emerged still capable of love, still reaching toward light, they find hope for their own journeys through whatever darkness currently holds them."

Sister Teresa eventually forbade visitors entirely for ten days, enforcing rest when my cough worsened and the inflammation of old scars became acute. I spent those days in my cell; the carved wooden figure Paolo had left at my door sitting on the windowsill where the morning light found it first.

He was permitted a brief visit on the third day of my confinement, entering my cell with the subdued reverence of one visiting a sacred space. His solemn eyes took in the medicines on the small table, the extra blankets despite June's warmth, the rosary beads draped over the bedpost, before settling on my face.

"You've been ill," he said.

“Yes. But recovering now.” I held up the carved figure. “Thank you for this. The habit must have been difficult work to make wood look like cloth.”

He flushed, pleased, and embarrassed. “It took many tries to get right.”

“You succeeded.” I set it down between us. “Will you sit for a moment?”

He sat, composed, watching me with the steadiness that had characterized him since our first meeting in the infirmary. Then, with the directness children bring to matters adults circle around: “Sister Teresa says you were coughing blood. Are you dying?”

“Not imminently,” I said. “My body remembers old wounds. Sometimes the remembering is more painful than others.”

He nodded. “Like my dreams about my mother. Sometimes they hurt more than other times.”

“Yes. Very much like that.”

A pause. Then: “I pray for you. Every night before sleep, and at Mass on Sundays.”

“I am honored by your prayers,” I said, and meant it in a way the words barely carried.

He accepted this and turned to the next matter on his mind with his characteristic directness. “Will you finish your story? Sister Giovanna says you are recording your life so others can learn from it.”

“Yes. There is not much left to write, just the later years, the coming to Schio, the finding of new purpose here.”

“Will I be in it?” A flicker of eagerness briefly crossed his solemn features.

“Would you like to be?”

He considered carefully. “Yes,” he decided. “So, others who read it will know that your coming here mattered. That you helped us too, not just the other way around.”

His perception startled me. The recognition that healing moves in both directions, that the exchange between one who has been wounded and one currently being wounded is never one-way, always mysterious in its circulation of giving and receiving.

"Then you shall be in it," I promised. "Though I may not use your name, to protect your privacy."

He accepted this with the practicality of one who understands that stories, once committed to paper, take on lives beyond either teller or subject. "That's sensible," he agreed. Then, noting Sister Teresa's approach down the corridor: "I should go. You need rest to heal properly."

"Your visit has been better medicine than her bitter draughts," I said. "Thank you for coming."

After he had gone, I sat holding the small wooden figure, feeling its smooth contours against my palm, its weight more substantial than its size suggested. Through the window, the garden was in full June abundance, the last of the spring flowers giving way to early summer's deeper color. The mountains stood behind it all, unhurried, present in the way that only very large and very permanent things can be.

I set the carved figure back on the windowsill where the morning light would find it first, and lay back against the pillow to rest as Sister Teresa had instructed.

The work was nearly finished. A few more sections remained. The later years, the coming to Schio, and this, whatever this was becoming. The strength would return, as it had before.

Outside, the garden moved in a light wind. The mountains held their position against the afternoon sky.

Chapter Nineteen

Winter came early to Schio that year. By late October, the frost had arrived in the valley, outlining each blade of grass and remaining leaf, and the mountains carried snow that crept lower each week, driving before it the sharp scent of pine and altitude when winds swept through.

It began with my hands.

The pain in my joints, which had come and gone for years, now settled in permanently. My fingers, once nimble enough to thread the finest needle or write the most delicate script, curled inward, stiff and unresponsive to what my mind requested of them.

"Rheumatism," said Sister Teresa, examining my hands. "Made worse by old injuries, poor circulation, and the mountain cold."

"Will it improve in spring?" I asked, already knowing the answer, but needing to hear it spoken.

She weighed truth against comfort. "Perhaps slightly," she said. "The warmth may bring some relief. But this is not a seasonal condition. It is progressive."

Progressive. The word implied things my mind understood but my spirit resisted. Not a temporary limitation, but the beginning of a journey deeper into physical constraint, a narrowing that might never reverse.

"I see," I said simply.

"I will prepare salves," she continued. "Warm compresses may help during the worst episodes. And we must consider how your duties might be adjusted."

Mother Francesca called me to her office the following day. The October sunlight slanted through her window, dust moving slowly in the still air. She gestured for me to sit, her eyes taking in the careful way I moved, the rigid curl of my fingers.

"Your narrative," she began. "Is it complete?"

"Nearly. I have written through my profession, my early years in Venice. Only my time here in Schio remains to be recorded."

"And your handwriting, it has become difficult, I imagine."

I looked down at my hands. "Yes. The writing is slower, less precise. Some days, holding the pen becomes impossible."

"Then we shall provide a scribe," she decided. "Sister Gabriella has a fine hand and a discreet nature. She will write as you dictate, completing what remains of your testimony."

The thought created momentary resistance, that my story might be finished through another's hand, that the private communion between memory and page might be shared with a third person. Then the resistance dissolved. My life had never been mine alone. It had always existed in relationship, been shaped by others' actions both cruel and kind, been witnessed by those who saw in my journey some reflection of universal human struggles toward dignity and meaning.

"Thank you," I said. "That is a generous solution."

Sister Gabriella came each morning, seating herself at a small desk beside my chair, her notebook open, her pen ready to capture what I could no longer write myself. She was young, perhaps twenty-five, with the combination of enthusiasm and solemnity often found in those newly professed. Her handwriting was elegant, her manner subdued, her eyes occasionally widening at certain passages, but her pen never faltering.

"You have experienced more in your life than most could imagine," she remarked one morning after writing a difficult passage describing my time in the branding house. "Yet you speak of these horrors with such composure."

"Time creates distance," I replied, though this was not entirely true. The memories remained vivid, immediate in ways that defied chronological remove. "And perspective, the ability to see even the darkest experiences as part of a larger pattern whose full design remains partially hidden from view."

She nodded, accepting this explanation, though certain understandings come only through direct experience of the extremities of human existence, and those cannot be communicated, only recognized by those who have traveled similar ground.

The narrative neared completion as November yielded to December, as the first heavy snows transformed Schio into a landscape of white silence broken only by church bells and the distant sounds of children delighting in winter's arrival. Sister Gabriella's notebook filled page by page with the final chapters: my arrival in Schio, my work with the children, my declining health and its unexpected opening into new forms of service.

"It feels strange," I confessed one morning as she prepared to write the concluding passages. "To be composing an ending while the story continues to unfold. To be speaking of decline while still experiencing its progression."

"Perhaps all memoirs share this quality," she suggested, her pen poised above fresh paper. "The living testimony is never truly complete while the witness remains to observe its ongoing development."

As autumn had deepened into winter, a wheelchair had been arranged, a sturdy construction from Vicenza that allowed me to move between rooms without walking, to continue receiving visitors and participating in the community's life on altered terms. Sister Lucretia, newly professed and strong in both frame and spirit, was appointed to assist with the transitions my condition now required.

"You speak of your body's limitations without bitterness," she remarked one morning after helping me through the washroom routine my condition now required, exposing in the process the full record of scars that mapped my torso, back, and limbs. "Many in your situation would be angry. At God, at circumstance."

"Anger is not always wrong," I told her. "I have felt it. But bitterness is anger that has turned inward and begun to consume what it was meant to protect. Between them lies a distinction worth attending to."

She received this seriously, as she received most things. "Nevertheless," she said, "you maintain a peace that seems to go beyond acceptance. Beyond simply enduring."

What she perceived as peace was not the absence of pain. The pain was constant, and as my body worsened it acquired new forms, the particular fire of inflamed nerves, the deep ache of swollen joints that Sister Teresa's salves could ease but never resolve. But over the years something had shifted in my relationship to that pain. Each morning before receiving visitors, each afternoon when the community gathered for prayer, I offered what came. Not as a transaction with God, not as spiritual accounting, but as the only thing remaining entirely within my freedom to give. *Lord, I offer this body with all its weaknesses and wounds. Use it as You will.*

The prayer did not transform pain into pleasure. But it altered my relation to what could not be changed, shifting it from affliction merely endured to something participated in, connected, through whatever mystery links human suffering to divine purpose, to the needs of those who continued to seek whatever I had been positioned to offer.

The visitors continued to come. A man arrived one bitter January day, the snow falling steadily outside my window. Sister Lucretia announced him simply as a visitor from Milan, respecting the anonymity that many preferred.

He entered carefully, his gaze taking in the wheelchair, the twisted hands resting in my lap, the body diminished by months of declining appetite and progressive weakness. Something in his expression shifted from uncertainty to recognition, though we had never met.

"You are as they described," he said, settling into the chair Sister Lucretia had positioned opposite mine. "Both more and less than I expected."

"Less in body, certainly," I acknowledged. "More in what way, I cannot say."

He did not return the small smile, his face remaining solemn in its controlled emotion. "I have come a long distance," he said. "Not only in physical miles, but in reluctance. I did not wish to be here."

"Yet here you are. Which suggests the journey, however unwelcome, held some necessity you recognized even as you resisted it."

He nodded, a sharp movement suggesting both agreement and ongoing conflict. "They say you understand suffering," he continued. "Not merely as concept, but as experienced reality. That you have known captivity, violation, the degradation of being treated as less than human."

"Yes. Those experiences are part of my history, though not the entirety of my story."

"Then perhaps you can answer a question that has haunted me for three years, that has robbed me of sleep and purpose, which has driven me to the edge of faith and sometimes beyond it." He leaned forward, his gaze direct. "How does one forgive the unforgivable? How does one continue to believe in a God who permits innocent suffering on an obscene scale? How does one live in a world where such things are not only possible but actual?"

I did not rush to answer, allowing the full weight of his questions to settle, to be acknowledged in their legitimate intensity. These were not abstract theological puzzles, but wounds as real as any physical injury.

"May I ask what prompts these questions?" I said finally. "Suffering takes particular forms that require particular responses. The general does not always reach the specific."

He hesitated, his hands clasping and unclasping. "My daughter," he said, the words emerging with visible effort. "She was taken in Albania three years ago. Not for ransom. For other purposes."

I nodded, understanding immediately what he could not bring himself to articulate; the particular horror of human trafficking, the specific violation of being treated as commodity rather than person.

"We found her," he continued, his voice dropping. "After eight months of searching, of bribing officials, of following every rumor and lead across three countries. We found her in a brothel in Tirana, so changed I might have passed her on the street without recognition."

He fell silent, the weight of it filling the room between us.

"She lives now in a convent in Switzerland," he said after a long pause. "The sisters there specialize in caring for girls rescued from such circumstances. She receives treatment. She is safe. She is cared for. She may, in time, recover some semblance of the girl she was before."

"But you have not recovered," I said quietly. "You remain captive to rage, to questions that admit no satisfying answer, to the torment of one who witnessed the aftermath but could not prevent the initial violation."

"Yes." The syllable contained volumes. "The priests tell me I must forgive in order to heal. The doctors suggest medication to dull the edges of what they call traumatic response. My wife has returned to church. She has found comfort in ritual and community that remains inaccessible to me. But I am frozen in that moment of recognition, of seeing my child so altered, so deeply wounded, and knowing that God, if He exists at all, allowed it to happen."

I did not reach for consolation. Whatever had been done to his daughter was evil. Whatever had been done to me was evil. Neither required softening into something more theologically comfortable.

"I cannot tell you why such things are permitted," I said finally. "I have asked that question myself, in darkness and in light, in captivity and in freedom. Why some are delivered and others not. Why some prayers seem answered and others met with silence. I have no answer that would satisfy either intellect or heart."

He nodded, accepting this honesty without surprise or disappointment. "Yet you continue to believe," he observed. "Despite all you have endured, all you have witnessed."

"Yes. Though not without struggle. Not without moments of doubt so profound they threatened to extinguish faith entirely. Not without questions that remain unanswered even now."

"Then what sustains you?" The question emerged with sudden intensity. "If not certainty, if not clear answers to these fundamental questions, what allows you to continue believing in the face of evidence that seems to argue powerfully for God's indifference?"

I took care with my answer, wanting to offer something that might actually touch his specific wound rather than rely on generalized wisdom.

"Two things," I said. "First, the impossibility of explanation is not the same as the absence of meaning. That I cannot comprehend the whole does not prove there is no whole to comprehend. Mystery and meaninglessness are not the same condition; however similar they feel in the depths of grief."

He nodded, not in agreement necessarily, but in acknowledgment of the distinction.

"And second," I continued, "the evidence of transformation. Not that suffering is good, or desired by God, or necessary to some cosmic calculation. But that what is intended to destroy can sometimes, through means I cannot explain and would not have predicted, become the ground from which something entirely new grows. Not because the wrong is made right by what follows, it is never made right, but because the last word in any human story has not yet been spoken."

He sat with this, his gaze shifting to the window where snow continued to fall. "And you believe it does not," he said finally. "Have the final word."

"I believe that what I have witnessed in my own life and in the lives of many who have sat in that chair suggests a pattern of redemption operating beneath and beyond the visible surface of events. Not as magical erasure of what has occurred. Not as cosmic pretense that violation never happened. But as genuine transformation of what seemed merely destructive into something that contains the possibility of new life, new purpose, new meaning beyond the boundaries of what suffering alone would dictate."

I paused, aware that abstract theology might fail to reach the specific wound this father carried. "Your daughter lives," I continued. "She is receiving care. She may recover some semblance of the girl she was before. But she will also be something new, not merely damaged or diminished, but potentially enlarged in ways neither you nor she can yet imagine. Not because of the harm done to her, but because of how she meets it, how you and those around her create something the people who used her never intended and cannot control."

He nodded more completely this time, as if something had reached a place that other explanations had not.

"You speak from experience," he said. "Not merely theory."

"Yes. From experience that includes both the depths of degradation and the heights of unexpected grace. From a life that has contained both the absolute negation of human dignity and its mysterious restoration through channels I could never have expected or engineered myself."

When our time drew to its close, when Sister Lucretia appeared discreetly at the door, he rose to leave with reluctance tinged by something that resembled, if not peace, then perhaps its precondition, the willingness to remain open to possibility beyond the boundaries of current perception.

"May I return?" he asked at the threshold. "If I find myself in need of further conversation?"

"Of course. Though I cannot promise how much longer this body will permit such exchanges. It seems determined to free itself from my use in increasingly direct ways."

Something eased in his solemn features. "You speak of your own decline with remarkable equanimity," he observed. "As if it were happening to someone else entirely."

"Not someone else," I said. "But not the entirety of who I am, either. This body has served faithfully through captivity and freedom alike. Its gradual surrender is not tragedy, but simply the last passage of a journey that began long before I understood its destination and continues beyond what I can currently perceive."

"Thank you," he said simply. "For your time, for your honesty, for your presence. It is a rare gift in a world more comfortable with explanation than witness."

Paolo came one September afternoon, the mountains brushed with autumn's first color, the garden giving its final flush before the long rest. Sister Teresa, recognizing the bond that had formed between this solemn boy and the dying nun, permitted a brief visit despite my increasingly non-responsive state.

He was thirteen now and growing, tall enough to stoop slightly when entering the room, his voice still catching him by surprise in its lower registers, his face suspended between childhood and whatever would follow it. He sat beside my bed; his hands folded in his lap in the posture of one accustomed to waiting quietly.

From his pocket he withdrew a small object wrapped in a handkerchief and placed it carefully in my open palm. A wooden rose, carved from pale wood polished to a warm glow, its petals rendered with remarkable attention, its stem complete with delicately carved thorns that pressed lightly against my sensitized skin.

"I've been carving again," he said, watching my face.

The rose lay in my curled hand, its weight precise and its thorns a reminder that beauty and pain share the same stem and do not require separation to be fully themselves.

"It is beautiful," I said. "You have a true gift."

He flushed, pleased and embarrassed in equal measure. Then, with the directness he had always brought to what mattered most: "I don't know if you can hear me properly. Sister Teresa says you might, even though you seem to sleep most of the time now."

He paused, then continued without waiting for a response that did not come.

"I wanted to thank you. For seeing me when others didn't. For listening when it mattered most. For showing me that loss isn't the end of the story but just a chapter that changes what comes afterward."

The room held the stillness of late afternoon, light slanting low and golden through the east-facing window, touching the small altar on the table beside my bed: the crucifix, the statue of the Madonna, the candles the sisters kept perpetually lit.

"I'll remember," he said, his voice steadying. "Not just what you said, but how you listened. Not just the stories you told, but the way you lived them. Not just the faith you talked about, but how you showed it was possible even when everything suggested otherwise."

He fell silent. The room filled with my labored breathing and the distant call of birds from the garden.

"Goodbye, Madre Moretta," he said, and rose to leave.

Winter returned. The mountains took the snow again and the garden went under.

By February the infirmary room had become my world, the east-facing window, the small altar, the sound of the sisters moving through their offices in the hours before dawn, the particular quality of winter light that arrived each morning and crossed the wall above my bed before the bell rang for Mass.

The rose Paolo had carved sat on the windowsill where the morning light found it first, its pale wood warm in the early sun, its thorns pressing lightly against nothing.

Outside, the mountains stood against the winter sky, their peaks carrying the particular quality of light that comes only in the cold months, precise, without shadow, permanent.

Chapter Twenty

The final days arrived without announcement.

Sister Teresa had been monitoring the change in my breathing for a week before she spoke of it to Mother Francesca, not within my cell, but in the corridor outside, her voice low and professional. She did not know that hearing, in those last weeks, had become the sharpest of my remaining senses, straining toward sound the way a plant in a dark room strains toward the single available window.

"The pneumonia has settled in both lungs," she said. "Given her already compromised breathing, I would not expect more than a few days. Perhaps a week."

Mother Francesca did not argue with the diagnosis or press for treatments that might briefly delay what had become clear to everyone. "Has she expressed any final wishes?" she asked instead. "Any instructions for after?"

"None beyond what she indicated years ago," Sister Teresa replied. "To be buried simply, without ceremony. To have her story preserved, but not published without proper Church review and approval. To be remembered, if at all, not as exceptional, but as evidence of grace working through the most ordinary of vessels."

A soft sound from Mother Francesca, not quite a laugh, but carrying the particular quality of one who recognizes irony without wishing to diminish it. "Ordinary," she repeated. "Perhaps the one thing Madre Moretta has never been, despite her constant insistence otherwise."

Their footsteps moved away down the corridor, their voices fading beyond my ability to follow.

News of my dying spread through the convent with the efficiency of close communities. Sisters came in ones and twos, standing briefly beside my bed, their whispered prayers forming a low, constant murmur at the edges of my awareness. Some wept quietly. Others kept the composed exterior that occasionally cracked to show what lay beneath. All touched me. A hand on my forehead, fingers briefly wrapped around my unresponsive ones, a palm resting lightly on my shoulder.

Sister Gabriella came and sat for longer periods, sometimes reading from my own narrative in a voice that broke occasionally, sometimes simply present in the silence between her rosary beads. "Your story will not be forgotten," she whispered once, believing me asleep. "Your witness will remain long after this room stands empty."

She was right, though not perhaps in the way she meant. The pages she had transcribed so faithfully, my careful dictation rendered in her elegant hand, would outlast both of us, would make their way into the world in forms neither of us could yet imagine.

Sister Lucretia came most often, turning my increasingly numb body, moistening lips too dry for speech, adjusting blankets with a tenderness that had long since passed beyond professional duty into something closer to love. "The townspeople are gathering," she told me one evening, her voice subdued. "In the chapel, in the courtyard, even in the street beyond the walls. Word has spread that you are leaving, and they come to keep watch."

I drifted between awareness and its absence, the fever painting landscapes of memory behind closed eyelids. Time lost its linear quality, becoming instead something circular, simultaneous, past and present moving together in overlapping currents.

I was a child in Olgossa, the red earth warm beneath bare feet, my mother's voice calling me home at dusk, my true name falling from her lips with the casual frequency of one who does not know that such ordinary usage will one day become impossible.

I was in the slave market, the weight of chains against raw skin, the assessing gaze of strangers moving over my body like physical touch, the complete negation of personhood that comes with such reduction.

I was a novice in Venice, the weight of rosary beads in fingers learning their pattern of prayer, the gradual transformation of identity that comes with discipline chosen freely rather than imposed by cruelty.

I was Madre Moretta in Schio, the weight of children's trust, the responsibility of receiving others' suffering without drowning in its depths.

All these and countless others moved through me in overlapping waves, not sequential but simultaneous, not past but present in a consciousness increasingly freed from time's ordinary constraints.

On the third day of what Sister Teresa had identified as the final decline, Mother Francesca made an unprecedented decision. "Open the doors," she told Sister Lucretia. "Allow those who wish to come and pay their respects to do so, briefly and in small groups. She has belonged to this community as much as to our order. They have the right to say goodbye."

They came. Shopkeepers and farmers, parents whose children I had taught, children now grown who remembered Madre Moretta from their schooldays. They came with flowers despite winter's dominion, with rosaries wrapped around work-roughened hands, with the quiet that people carry when they understand they are present at something that will not happen again.

Paolo came with his father. He was seventeen now, his frame filled out from the lanky boy of recent years into the solid presence of the man he was becoming. He stood beside the bed for a long moment without speaking, his hands folded in the posture of one accustomed to waiting quietly.

When a journalist later asked what had made Madre Moretta significant in his life, his answer was simple and direct, as his answers had always been.

"She saw me," he said. "Not just my presence, but my struggles, my specific needs, my essential self beneath whatever surface I presented to the world. She listened when others merely heard, recognized what others overlooked, offered what others withheld."

"The bishop has come," Sister Lucretia whispered on the fourth morning, her voice reaching me through the deepening fog. "He wishes to give you a final blessing."

His presence entered the room, that combination of authority and uncertainty that often characterizes those in positions of power when confronted with mysteries that transcend institutional categories. His blessing fell like rain, the words indistinguishable but the intention clear, offering final benediction to one whose journey had begun far from any church's boundaries yet had somehow illuminated possibilities central to its most authentic mission.

Morning light was entering the room when Sister Teresa spoke to Mother Francesca in a voice she no longer troubled to lower. "Her breathing pattern has changed. The rattle has deepened. These are the final stages."

Her voice seemed to come from a great distance. Yet other sounds grew clearer, not vibrations of air but something that required no such medium. My mother's voice, calling my true name. My sister's laughter beneath the great baobab. The Woman in White, whose presence I had first known in desert dreams, who had visited my cell during the dark night of the soul in this very convent, who had been a constant companion throughout the years of physical surrender. She was present now, at the boundary between here and what lay beyond it.

I had been carried across deserts, sold in markets, branded in cellar rooms, freed in courtrooms, baptized in chapels, professed in candlelight, reduced to stillness in this small bed beside this east-facing window. The journey had begun in darkness and in song simultaneously, in loss and in belonging, and had moved through every variation of both without resolution into either alone.

The Woman in White waited with the patience of one who exists beyond time's ordinary constraints. Simply present, as she had always been, at the place where the path led.

My lips, dry from fever and disuse, formed the words that required no voice to carry them across the room.

"Our Lady. Our Lady."

Not a prayer. Not a petition. A recognition. The greeting of one who has reached, after long traveling, the face that had been present at every point along the way without being visible until now.

The last door opened.

Sister Teresa leaned forward. Straightened. Her face held the gravity of one who has attended many such transitions and approaches each one with undiminished respect.

"She is gone," she said simply.

Mother Francesca made the sign of the cross, her movements precise despite the emotion visible in her usually composed face. "May she rest in peace."

"Amen," responded the gathered sisters, their voices filling the small room.

They buried her four days later in the small cemetery beside the convent, as she had requested, without elaborate ceremony, without excess.

February's cold held the earth still hard. The bishop who had given the final blessing presided over the funeral rites, his Latin prayers rising into air sharp with cold and the particular clarity that comes after prolonged snowfall. The sisters sang the ancient chants that mark such transitions, their voices weaving harmonies that carried across the cemetery wall and into the streets beyond.

The people of Schio gathered around the grave. Shopkeepers and factory workers, farmers and housewives, children and elderly, those who had sat in the parlor chair across from her and those who had only heard her name spoken with a particular quality of reverence. They stood in silence as the coffin was lowered into the earth. They remained after the official rites concluded, offering private prayers, leaving flowers that the cold would quickly take, creating through their collective presence the kind of testimony that no official record fully captures.

Paolo stood at the graveside with his father, his face composed, his eyes carrying what they had always carried, that depth of one who has known loss early and learned to hold it without being defined by it.

The convent bell rang across the valley, its sound crossing the rooftops and carrying out toward the mountains. The mountains stood where they had always stood, unhurried, present, indifferent to season and to human grief alike, their peaks sharp against the February sky.

A single candle burned in the window of the infirmary room, visible from the cemetery.

The rose Paolo had carved sat on the windowsill beside it, its pale wood catching the winter light.

Saint Josephine Bakhita

Biography

Feast Day: February 8

Birth: c. 1869, Darfur, Sudan

Death: February 8, 1947, Schio, Italy

Canonization: October 1, 2000 by Pope John Paul II

Patronage: Sudan, human trafficking survivors, victims of slavery, refugees, the vulnerable, and those who suffer abuse

Saint Josephine Bakhita was born in Darfur, Sudan around 1869. At age seven, she was kidnapped by Arab slave traders, who gave her the name "Bakhita" meaning "fortunate." She was sold and resold in slave markets, enduring traumatic physical abuse and forceful conversion to Islam. She bore 144 scars from her enslavement for the rest of her life.

In 1883, she was purchased by an Italian consul, Callisto Legnani, who treated her with kindness. When Legnani returned to Italy, Bakhita asked to go with him. In Italy, she was given to the Michieli family, becoming the nanny to their daughter. When the family had to travel to Sudan for business, they left Bakhita and their daughter with the Canossian Sisters in Venice.

There, Bakhita encountered Christianity and received religious instruction. When the Michielis returned to claim her, Bakhita refused to leave. Italian courts ruled that since slavery was illegal in Italy, she had never legally been a slave there. Finally free, she chose to remain with the Canossians.

On January 9, 1890, Bakhita was baptized, taking the name Josephine Margaret. Three years later, she entered the novitiate with the Canossian Daughters of Charity and took her final vows on December 8, 1896.

She spent the next 50 years serving her community with humility as a cook, seamstress, and doorkeeper at the convent in Schio. Despite the painful memories of her enslavement, she was known for her gentle voice, kindness, and perpetual smile. When asked what she would do if she met her captors, she famously replied, "I would kneel and kiss their hands, for if these things had not happened, I would not have been a Christian and a religious today."

During her final illness, her mind often returned to her enslavement, crying out "Please, loosen the chains... they are so heavy!" She died on February 8, 1947.

Pope John Paul II beatified her on May 17, 1992, and canonized her on October 1, 2000. She is venerated as a model of Christian forgiveness and perseverance through suffering. Her life exemplifies how chains of bondage can transform into spiritual freedom through faith and love.

With Gratitude

Thank you for journeying with me through Saint Josephine Margaret Bakhita's tumultuous life. Bringing her story from the shadows of history into your hands has been a labor of love that consumed years of research, countless revisions, and an unwavering commitment to honoring the truth of her extraordinary existence.

If this novel moved you—whether it sparked outrage at the injustices Josephine endured, compassion for her impossible choices, or simply kept you turning pages late into the night, I would be deeply grateful if you would consider leaving a review. As an independent historical novelist, reader reviews are the lifeblood of my work. They help other readers discover stories like Josephine's that might otherwise remain forgotten. Each review, no matter how brief, amplifies voices from the past that deserve to be heard and helps me continue unearthing these hidden histories.

Your honest thoughts matter more than you might realize. A few sentences about what resonated with you, which characters captured your imagination, or how this story changed your perspective can make all the difference to both fellow readers searching for their next book and to authors like me who pour our hearts into illuminating these forgotten corners of history. Reviews on Amazon, Goodreads, or wherever you discovered this book help ensure that more stories of remarkable women like Josephine Bakhita find their way into the world.

Thank you for reading, for caring about these historical voices, and for helping keep their stories alive.

With gratitude,

Mirella Patzer

About the Author

Mirella Patzer is a Canadian author who brings the rich tapestry of Italian history to life through compelling historical fiction. Drawing upon her heritage as a first-generation Italian Canadian, she crafts authentic stories that bridge the gap between past and present.

Based in Calgary, Alberta, Mirella has always been captivated by the courage, passion, and resilience of individuals navigating the complexities of their times. Her deep connection to Italian culture, combined with meticulous research, allows her to create immersive worlds where readers can experience the atmosphere and emotions of historical Italy. Her work explores themes of justice, survival, and the enduring power of truth, while celebrating the strength of women who refuse to be silenced.

When not writing, Mirella enjoys researching the hidden stories that continue to inspire her work. She can often be found spending time with her family, cooking, reading, or enjoying a good dose of Netflix.

For more information about Mirella Patzer and her upcoming releases, visit www.mirellapatzer.com or follow her on Facebook, Instagram, TikTok, and Threads

www.ingramcontent.com/pod-product-compliance
Lightning Source LLC
LaVergne TN
LVHW091115080826
845145LV00008B/1919

* 9 7 8 1 9 9 8 1 6 9 5 3 5 *